MISSIONARY IN CONFUCIAN GARB

穿儒服的传教士

朱 菁 编著
Translated by Andrea Lee

五洲传播出版社
China Intercontinental Press

图书在版编目（CIP）数据

穿儒服的传教士：汉英对照/朱菁编著；（新加坡）李燕萍（Andrea Lee）译.—北京：五洲传播出版社，2010.1
　ISBN 978-7-5085-1718-6

Ⅰ.①穿…　Ⅱ.①朱…②李…　Ⅲ.①利玛窦（1552～1610）-生平事迹-汉、英②文化交流-文化史-汉、英　Ⅳ.①B979.954.6

中国版本图书馆CIP数据核字（2009）第192690号

中外文化交流故事丛书（Roads to the World）

总 策 划：许　琳
策　　划：马箭飞　孙文正　王锦红
顾　　问：赵启正　沈锡麟　潘　岳
　　　　　周黎明（美）李　莎（加）威廉·林赛（英）
出 版 人：荆孝敏　邓锦辉
编 著 者：朱　菁
翻　　译：Andrea Lee（新加坡）
项目统筹：邓锦辉
责任编辑：苏　谦
设计指导：田　林
封面绘画：李　骐
设计制作：北京尚捷时迅文化艺术有限公司
图　　片：Fotoe　CFP

穿儒服的传教士
Missionary in Confucian Garb

出版发行　五洲传播出版社（北京市海淀区北小马厂6号　邮编：100038）
电　　话　8610-58891281（发行部）
网　　址　www.cicc.org.cn
承 印 者　北京外文印务有限公司
版　　次　2010年1月第1版第1次印刷
开　　本　720×965毫米　1/16
印　　张　9.75
定　　价　76.00元

Contents 目 录

Foreword *4*

I. Matteo Ricci's Passage to China *8*

II. The Establishment of the Catholic Movement *34*

III. The Long-awaited Entrance to Beijing *60*

IV. Taking Root in Beijing *84*

V. Connecting the East and West through Friendship *102*

VI. Burial in Beijing *120*

VII. The Question of Rites *132*

前 言 *6*

1. 千辛万险，初抵中国 *9*

2. 改着儒服，开拓基业 *35*

3. 辗转反复，终入皇城 *61*

4. 皇帝上宾，扎根京城 *85*

5. 广交朋友，汇通中西 *103*

6. 赐葬北京，永留中华 *121*

7. 身后困惑，礼仪之争 *133*

FOREWORD

It has been a long and exciting history of tremendous cultural exchange between China and other countries. In terms of culture, economy, ideology, and personnel, these exchanges between China and other countries can be dated back to the times of Qin and Han dynasties—directly or indirectly, by land or sea. The long-term and multi-faceted cultural exchange helps the world to understand more about China and the rest of the world, enriching the common wealth of mankind—both materially and spiritually.

The book series entitled *Roads to the World* offers the most splendid stories in the entire history of Sino-foreign cultural exchange. We hereby offer them to foreign students learning the Chinese language, and to foreign readers who have a keen interest in Chinese culture. These stories depict important personalities, events, and phenomena in various fields of cultural exchange between China and other nations, and among different peoples. By reading the books, you may understand China and Chinese civilization profoundly, and the close link between Chinese civilization and other civilizations of the world. The books highlight the efforts and contributions of Chinese people and Chinese civilization in the world's cultural interchange. They reflect mankind's common spiritual pursuit and the orientation of values.

This book is about the Italian Jesuit, Matteo Ricci, who had traveled to China in the 16th century as a missionary, and lived in the country for 28 years until his death. It is a story of his efforts and achievements in facilitating the cultural exchange between the East and West. Matteo Ricci was committed and diligent in learning Chinese culture, and he assimilated himself successfully into China's society. In the process, he introduced Western scientific knowledge to the Chinese people, and also introduced Chinese culture to the Westerners. *The Journals of Matteo Ricci in China* is known to be a fundamental literary work that introduced China to the Westerners. Matteo Ricci was reputed as the Father of China's Catholicism, and the pioneer of Western's Chinese Studies. He is hailed as the role model in the history cultural exchange between the East and West.

前　言

　　中国与其他国家、民族之间的文化交流具有悠久而曲折的历史。在中国与外国之间，通过间接的和直接的、陆路的和海路的、有形的和无形的多种渠道，各种文化、经济、思想、人员方面的交流，可以上溯至秦汉时代，下及于当今社会。长期的、多方面的交流，增进了中国与其他国家、民族之间的了解，使人类的共同财富（物质的和精神的）更加丰富。

　　中外文化交流故事丛书（Roads to the World）的宗旨，是从中外文化交流的历史长河中，选择那些最璀璨的明珠，通过讲故事的方式，介绍给学习汉语的外国学生和对中国文化感兴趣的外国读者。这些故事描述中国与其他国家、民族在各个领域文化交流中的重要人物、事件和现象，以使外国读者能够更深入地理解中国，理解中国文明，理解中国文明与其他各文明之间的密切关系，以及中国人和中国文明在这种交流过程中所作出的努力和贡献，并尽力彰显人类共同的精神追求与价值取向。

本书讲述的是意大利传教士利玛窦于16世纪末来到中国，在中国生活28年，积极推动中西间文化交流的故事。利玛窦努力学习中国文化，融入中国社会，向中国人介绍西方科学知识，同时向西方人介绍中国文化。他的《利玛窦中国札记》被公推为西方人认识中国的基本著作。利玛窦本人则被誉为中国天主教之父、西方汉学的创始人，更有人赞他为中西文化交流史上的"最高典范"。

I

Matteo Ricci's Passage to China

For those who are familiar with cultural exchanges between the East and West, the name Matteo Ricci is no stranger to them. In one of his popular portraits, he dons a Confucian hat, a long, silvery white beard, looking stern, yet kind. He has the tall nose and deep-set eyes that are typical of a European, and his farsight and deep look in the eyes seem to utter a prayer, and penetrate into the soul of a mortal.

In the history of civilization, Matteo Ricci is like a massive bridge, facilitating the cultural between the East and West, satisfying the wish of the people of the two poles to know more about one another. Hence, he is hailed as "the predecessor of East-West cultural exchange."

In 1552, Matteo Ricci was born to a distinguished family in the city of Macerata in Italy. His family was the owner of a renowned pharmacy, which had been passed down for generations. His father, Giovanni Battista Ricci, was

1

千辛万险，初抵中国

熟悉中西文化交流史的人，对利玛窦（Matteo Ricci）这个名字都不会陌生。在一张流传很广的利玛窦画像上，他头戴高高的儒士帽，下巴上留着银白的长须，面容清癯，神态慈祥，高鼻深目显示出他的欧罗巴人种特征，睿智、深远的目光似乎在向天主告求，又仿佛能洞穿凡人的灵魂。

在世界文明史上，利玛窦如同一座宏伟的桥梁，促进了中西文化的往来，满足了东西方人民互相认识的愿望。他因而被称为"沟通中西文化第一人"。

1552年，利玛窦出生于意大利玛切拉塔城的一个显贵家庭，家里世代经营着著名的药店。父亲乔瓦尼·巴蒂斯塔·利奇（Giovanni Battista Ricci）是当地的市长，还曾经代理过安柯那省的省长。母亲乔瓦娜·安焦莱莉（Gionanna Angilelli）是一位侯爵的后裔。利玛窦是

the city mayor, and was once the provincial governor of Ancona. His mother, Gionanna Angilelli's family was a duke of Custer Falvey Keogh. Matteo Ricci was the eldest son, and had six younger siblings. The mayor envisioned Matteo to inherit his business. Since he was born, he had wanted to groom Matteo to become a politician. Hence, when Matteo was a young child, he was sent to a missionary school to be educated.

As Matteo Ricci had shown remarkable talent when he was a child, and was also a diligent student, his teacher thought highly of him. His teacher was one of the early Jesuits. Under his tutelage, the young Matteo Ricci came under an early influence of the Jesuits. When he was in junior school, Macerata was visited of more than a dozen Jesuit priests. They taught Matteo Ricci Latin, Greek and memory techniques. Matteo Ricci performed remarkably well in school, which delighted his father, who was hoping to see his son achieving great success in life and was arranging to send Matteo to study in a theology college in Rome.

In 1568, the 16 year-old Matteo Ricci went to Rome and studied law in college. However, Matteo was more interested in studying the Jesuit religion. Three years later, he discontinued his studies in law, and against his father's wish, decided to dedicate his life to God, and became a Jesuit like his teachers.

利玛窦像
Portrait of Matteo Ricci.

家中的长子，下面还有六个兄弟姐妹。市长大人一心期望大儿子能够继承他的事业，从利玛窦呱呱落地起，就想把他培养成一位政治家。利玛窦才几岁，就被父母送入教会学校学习。

由于利玛窦从小就显露出过人的天资，又十分勤奋，启蒙老师冯奇凡尼神父十分器重他。冯奇凡尼神父是早期的耶稣会士之一，在他的精心教导下，年幼的利玛窦与耶稣会结下了最初的渊源。当利玛窦进入小学阶段，属于教皇领土的玛切拉塔城又迎来了十几位耶稣会士，他们教授给利玛窦拉丁文、希腊文以及博闻强识的记忆术。

利玛窦在学校里的出众表现，让一心期待儿子出人头地的父亲欣喜万分，打算只待儿子中学毕业，就送他去罗马的法学院深造，为将来步入仕途打下良好的基础。

1568年，16岁的利玛窦进入罗马的圣汤多雷亚学院

On 15 August 1571, which was the Assumption of the Virgin Mary, Matteo Ricci officially joined the Jesuits. The following year, he began his studies at the Roman College, which was started by the Jesuits. The Roman College was a prestigious school which many students wanted to study in. Among the brilliant teachers of Matteo Ricci, the famous Mathematician Christopher Klau taught him mathematics and astronomy, and Alessandro Valignani, who became the Jesuit Far Eastern Inspector later, taught him theology and philosophy. Matteo Ricci continued his studies in Latin and Greek, and he also mastered the Portuguese and Spanish languages.

After five years of his college education, Matteo Ricci excelled in Mathematics, rhetoric, astronomy, geography and mechanics. By then, he was clear of his objective in life, that is, to travel to China in the Far East, and spread the gospels.

In 1577, the chief of the Jesuits gave Matteo Ricci the approval to travel to the Far East to spread the Christian faith. The following spring, Matteo Ricci, along with Michele Ruggieri, Francis Pasio and more than a dozens Jesuits, left for Lisbon, Portugal.

Matteo Ricci and his team of Jesuits visited the king of Portugal, and upon receiving his consent and sponsorship, they departed Lisbon on a Portuguese sailboat. The boat sailed past the Cape of Good Hope and Mozambique, and

学习法律预科。然而，自幼接受耶稣会教育的利玛窦早就立下了更加高远的目标。三年后，他没有遵从父亲的意愿继续攻读法律课程，而是决心献身上帝，像他的老师们那样成为卓越的耶稣会士。

1571年8月15日，正是圣母升天节。就在那一天，利玛窦终于如愿加入了耶稣会，成为一名耶稣会士。

第二年，他开始在耶稣会主办的罗马学院学习。罗马学院名师荟萃，是全欧洲学子都向往的名校。利玛窦的老师中有著名的数学家克拉乌（Christopher Klau），还有后来成为耶稣会远东巡视使的范礼安（Alessandro

16世纪末欧洲人眼中的中国人
The Chinese perceived by the Europeans in the 16th century.

six months later, arrived in a scorching hot Goa, India, in September.

In this first-ever voyage that he had undertaken, the toil that he had to endure far surpassed Matteo Ricci's imagination. The sailboat was not only small and cramped, but also unbearably hot when the air was completely still. Many time, the passengers found themselves breathless. The worst happened when a communicable disease broke out in this horrific environment, and 13 slaves, out of the 400 that boarded the boat, died. Matteo Ricci was lucky to not contract the disease, but by the time he reached Goa, he was so weak that it took him several months to regain his health.

Goa was Portugal's most important colony in Asia. Prior to his visit to Goa, Matteo Ricci had read many positive accounts of India by the Jesuits. Therefore, he felt that it would be rather easy for missionary work to take place there. But the India that he saw was far different from the one he read of before. In 1580, Matteo Ricci reported his observations to the Jesuit headquarters, remarking that many accounts of India and Japan, as well as their maps, were incredibly contrary to what had been written. What disappointed Matteo Ricci the most was that the Indians were totally uninterested in Christianity. It occurred to him that it would be a long and arduous task in spreading the faith throughout the

穿儒服的传教士

Valignani），他负责教授神学和哲学知识。此外，利玛窦进一步学习了拉丁文和希腊文，还学会了使用葡萄牙语和西班牙语。

经过五年的刻苦努力，利玛窦在数学、修辞学、天文学、地理学、机械学等各门课程中都取得了优异的成绩。此时的他，已经为自己确立了更加明确的目标——去远东，去中国，传播上帝的福音！

1577年，耶稣会总会长批准了利玛窦前往远东

16世纪欧洲人绘制的中国地图
A 16th-century map of China illustrated by the Europeans.

Missionary in Confucian Garb

16世纪的葡萄牙里斯本港口。1578年3月，利玛窦和其他14名耶稣会士一起，乘船从里斯本出发前往远东。
16th-century port of Lisbon, Portugal. In March 1578, Matteo Ricci and 14 Jesuits set off to the East from here.

Far East. However, the consolation was that missionary works in Japan was going on rather smoothly, and there were believers under the Catholic Nestorian missionary movement. Matteo Ricci and fellow missionaries were therefore very encouraged by the fact, and it strengthened their belief that they would achieve eventual success.

In India and Cochin (present-day northern Vietnam), Matteo Ricci spent four years in missionary work. He also

传教的申请。第二年春暖花开时节，利玛窦与罗明坚（Michele Ruggleri）、巴范济（Francis Pasio）等其他十几位耶稣会士一道，动身前往葡萄牙首都里斯本。

在当时，葡萄牙享有远东地区保教权。凡是从教皇国出发的传教士，都必须要前往里斯本，在葡萄牙国王那里领取护照，然后才能继续向东方进发。

利玛窦和罗明坚一行人拜见过葡萄牙国王，获得他的允许和资助后，乘坐一艘葡萄牙帆船，从里斯本出发，绕过好望角，经过莫桑比克，半年后，终于在炎热的9月到达了印度果阿。

生平第一次远航，路途的辛苦远远超过了利玛窦的想象。帆船的船舱又小又矮，没有风的时候，舱里酷热难耐，他们常常连气都喘不过来。更可怕的是，恶劣的环境引发了传染病，船上来自莫桑比克的400名奴隶中死去了13名。虽然侥幸没染上疫病，但利玛窦到达果阿时已极度虚弱，休息了几个月才恢复过来。

印度果阿是葡萄牙在亚洲最重要的殖民地。来之前，利玛窦读过很多耶稣会士关于印度的赞美文字，这让他以为，要在那里传教不会是特别困难的事情。可当他真正来到印度，才发现现实和原来的设想相差很大。

completed his studies in theology when he was in Goa. In July 1580, Matteo Ricci was ordained as a priest.

Based on his own experience as a missionary for the past few years, Matteo Ricci leant that the way to advance his missionary successful was to lead the locals to better understand Western cultures through the study of philosophy, catechism, and theology. Inspired by the thought, he communicated his ideas to the Jesuits Headquarters in a letter. He wrote that the Christian converts would not be able to claim a dominant role in society if they were not educated, neither would they be proud to be Christians. On the contrary, they might even feel that their newfound faith would come in the way of their pursuits in society. If not, he asserted, they would never be able to meet the objective of their missionary work in India, and would fail in converting the local people to Christianity.

These early opinions that were formed in Matteo Ricci's mind would accompany him throughout his entire life. He stood by his beliefs even when he came to China. The four years in India and Cochin had laid a solid foundation to his later missionary work in China.

One day in 1582, Matteo Ricci and his mission received an instruction from the Jesuit inspector, Father Alessandro Valignani, to leave India and set off to Macau, China.

From India, Matteo Ricci and his fellow Jesuit began a

1580年，利玛窦非常困惑地向耶稣会总部汇报："我仔细地对照了有关印度、日本的书籍注释和地图，结果发现，明显的谬误现象简直太普遍了。"尤其令利玛窦感到失望的是，印度人对于他们所带来的神学似乎毫无兴趣。看来要让上帝的福音之花开遍远东，还需要经过一段曲折的过程。不过，由于当时耶稣会在日本的传教事业进展得十分顺利，而且在印度又发现了天主教聂斯托里派的信徒，所以利玛窦和同伴们还是被希望和激情鼓舞，相信会有天国的光明照亮他们的事业。

在印度和交趾（今越南北部），利玛窦先后度过了四年的传教生活。他一边传播福音，一边在果阿的神学院继续此前没有完成的学业。1580年7月，利玛窦晋升为司铎。

通过几年来传教的亲身经历，利玛窦意识到，如果能引导当地人学习哲学、教理和神学等课程，了解欧洲文化，会让传教事业进展得更加顺利。于是，他满怀热忱地给耶稣会总部写信，提出了自己的看法。他在信里说，如果不让想入教的人成为更有文化的人，他们就没有办法在社会上取得较高的地位、担任有权力的职务，也就感受不到身为教徒的荣耀，甚至会觉得入教阻碍了

Missionary in Confucian Garb

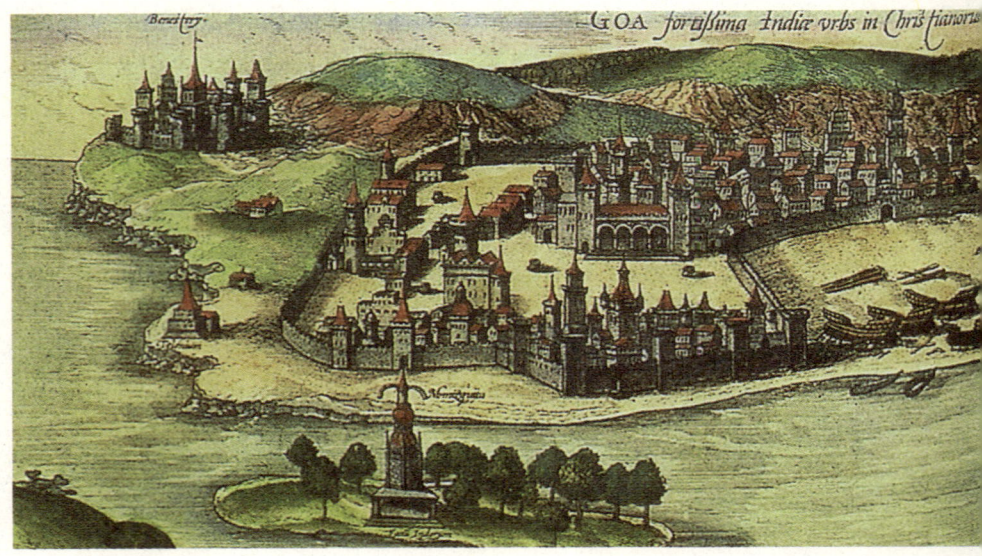

long and arduous voyage to China. Matteo Ricci almost died during the journey due to an illness. In August 1582, they finally arrived in Macau, which was the window to which they would know more about China.

Since the early 16th century, the Portuguese had been trading with the Chinese. Later, on the pretext that they needed to sun their merchandise on land, the Portuguese started building houses in Macau and living there. When Matteo Ricci and his mission arrived in Macau, most of the foreigners they saw were Portuguese. As the Ming Dynasty (1368–1644) had imposed a seclusion policy, the Portuguese could only trade in Guangzhou from Macau during a specific period every year. Gradually,

穿儒服的传教士

16世纪的印度果阿。利玛窦在果阿和交趾传教四年，1582年从果阿出发前往中国澳门。
16th-century Goa, India. Matteo Ricci preached in Goa for four years before leaving for Macau, China in 1582.

他们跻身上层社会。这样的话，耶稣会在印度的主要目的就没有办法达到，感化异教徒并使他们皈依上帝、树立神圣信仰的使命将会化为泡影。

早年间形成的这些见解伴随了利玛窦一生。后来他进入中国后，仍然始终坚持同样的态度。印度和交趾的四年，为利玛窦日后在中国的传教事业打下了很好的基础。

1582年的一天，罗明坚、利玛窦和巴范济收到了耶稣会远东巡查使范礼安的命令：离开印度，前赴中

Macau began to develop into an important trading centre between China and Europe.

Before the arrival of Matteo Ricci and his mission, the Jesuits had already been living in the Macau for over 30 years. The prohibition of the Ming government had prevented them from entering Mainland China. These missionaries did not understand Chinese, and was ill-informed about China's politics. In an attempt to change the situation, Father Alessandro Valignani ,who supervised the Jesuit missions in the Far East, instructed Matteo Ricci and his fellow missionaries to master the Chinese language and to learn more about the cultures and lifestyles of the Chinese people. They must also strive to achieve a breakthrough in the Ming government's prohibition of foreigners into China, and to enter Beijing as soon as they could.

In Macau, Matteo Ricci spent most of his time learning the Chinese language. He was greatly baffled by the Chinese characters and phonics, which were totally different from the West's. He hired a Chinese teacher to teach him in mastering the language, while in actual fact, no Chinese were allowed to teach the foreigners Chinese. However, Matteo Ricci's Chinese teacher was greatly impressed by his sincerity and determination, and took the risk in accepting this foreign student.

Initially, Matteo Ricci would draw out what he

16世纪的澳门。1565年,耶稣会在此设立了澳门学院,负责管理中国和日本的传教事务。
16th-century Macau. In 1565, the Jesuits established the Macau Institute, taking charge of all missionary matters in China and Japan.

国澳门。

从印度前往中国的海上旅行漫长而艰险,途中的一场急病差点让利玛窦丢掉性命。1582年8月,利玛窦一行抵达澳门。这里将成为他们了解中国的窗口。

16世纪初,葡萄牙人就开始与中国通商。后来,他们借口要上岸晒货,在澳门建屋聚居。当利玛窦他们来到澳门时,在这里的外国人仍然主要是葡萄牙人。由于明朝(1368—1644)政府实行闭关锁国的政策,葡萄牙商人每年只能在规定的时间从澳门前往广州进行贸易。澳门渐渐发展为当时欧洲与中国之间最重要的贸易中心。

encountered in his day-to-day living. His Chinese teacher would then write out the Chinese words based on his drawings, and taught him how to read them. Once Matteo Ricci's vocabulary had increased, his teacher would teach him some simple sentences. Compare to Michele Ruggieri, who was reaching 40, the younger Matteo Ricci found it rather easy to pick up the language. However, it did not mean that the process was altogether an easy task, especially when he came to the four-tone pronunciation of the Chinese words. Unheard of in the West, it was mind-boggling for Matteo Ricci. If he made a mistake in the tone of the word, the meaning of it would change drastically. For a foreigner to master the distinction of the four tones, it would require a lot of hard work. But in order to adequately understand Chinese culture, Matteo Ricci was determined to master the skill, word by word.

Before long, Matteo Ricci's started to show progress in the Chinese language, to the extent of understanding the confessions of the local people. He went on to attempt conversing in Mandarin, and was able to read some simple Chinese texts. He progressed to practicing writing in Chinese, so as to use it to spread the gospels to the Chinese people in future.

Matteo Ricci and Michele Ruggieri tried to seize every possible opportunity to go further into China, and fulfill their mission. Over three occasions, they followed

在利玛窦一行到达澳门的30多年前，就已有传教士在那里生活。由于明朝政府的限制，在澳门的西方传教士始终无法进入中国内地。这些传教士既不懂中文，对中国国情也知之甚少。耶稣会远东巡视使范礼安急于改变这种状况。他在离开澳门去日本巡视前，特意留下信件，指示罗明坚和利玛窦一定要学好中国语言和文字，熟悉中国的风土人情，并设法突破明朝政府的禁令，争取尽早进入北京。

在澳门的日子里，利玛窦花费了大量的时间学习中国语文。与西方拼音文字完全不同的方块汉字，令他感到非常不可思议。他专门请了一位中国老师教他学习汉语。实际上，明朝政府严禁中国人向外国人传授汉语，利玛窦凭着满腔热诚和执著打动了中国老师，使他冒险收下了这位外国学生。

刚开始，利玛窦将平时在生活中能够接触到的东西都画出来，他的中国老师按照这些图画给他写出中文，再教他读出这些词。当利玛窦的词汇量增加以后，老师再教他学习简单的汉语句子。比起已经快40岁的罗明坚，年轻的利玛窦学习起来要稍微轻松些。但整个学习过程依然非常艰苦，尤其是汉语中的四声问题，这是他

Portuguese traders into Guangzhou, and made contacts with the local officials there. Matteo Ricci left a very good impression to the local officials, who all thought of him as a foreign teacher, as well as a priest with a gentle demeanor and a considerable amount of learning in the Chinese culture.

In December 1582, with the assistance of Chen Rui, the Governor-General of Guangzhou, Michele Ruggieri was given an approval to visit Zhaoqing, located in the Midwestern part of Guangdong. There, he stayed for several months in a Buddhist monastery, Tianning Monastery. Later, Chen Rui was dismissed from his duty, and Michele Ruggieri was ordered to return to Macau. When the new governor, Guo Ying, took office, he saw the application that Michele Ruggieri had submitted to build a monastery in Zhaoqing. Upon discussion with Wang Pan, the prefecture magistrate of Zhaoqing, he approved this application, and sent his men to invite Michele Ruggieri back to Zhaoqing.

It was a once-in-a-lifetime opportunity that Michele Ruggieri and Matteo Ricci had been yearning for. They immediately made the necessary preparation, and in the summer of 1583, they set off to Zhaoqing.

At the Zhaoqing magistrate's office, the two foreigners paid respect to the magistrate in accordance to the rites and etiquettes of the Chinese people, to which the

在西方语言里从来没有遇到过的，令他十分头疼。在汉语中，同样的发音音调不同，意思就完全不一样了。对于外国人来说，要在有限的时间里掌握好四声的区别，实在需要大费周折。但为了更好地了解中国文化，利玛窦像小学生那样，坚持一字一句地学习。

很快，利玛窦的汉语水平有了明显提高。他已经可以倾听当地人用汉语做的忏悔，接着又学会了用汉语会话和进行简单的阅读。利玛窦决定进一步练习汉语写作，争取将来能够用汉语向中国人传播天主教教义。

罗明坚和利玛窦在澳门还积极寻求机会，以便进入中国内地，完成范礼安交待的任务。他们先后三次跟随葡萄牙商人进入广州，在与中国地方官员的接触中，给这些官员留下了很好的印象，被认为是文质彬彬的君子和有中国文学修养的外国神父。

1582年12月，在两广总督陈瑞的帮助下，罗明坚获准进入位于广东中西部的肇庆，在当地的一所佛教寺院天宁寺住了好几个月。后来，因为陈瑞被免职，罗明坚不得不回到澳门。

新总督郭应聘到任后，发现了罗明坚此前申请"拨地建寺筑舍"的文件。郭总督和肇庆知府王泮商量后，

magistrate return accordingly. After which, the magistrate started to investigate their backgrounds.

Michele Ruggieri and Matteo Ricci explained that they were monks who served God, and had traveled a long distance to visit China, as they were great admirers of the Chinese culture. They hoped to find a plot of pristine land in Zhaoqing to build their church, and to remain in China till death. They would not marry or form family for ever, and would instead dedicate their entire lives in God's service. This was the way they phrased it as they knew that under the Ming government's decree, foreigners who wanted to reside in China were not allowed to return to their own countries. They were also not allowed to take Chinese women out of the country, or they would be severely punished. Of course, they could not be direct in expressing that they were in China to convert the Chinese to Catholicism, which would equally land them outside China.

Seeing that they were sincere, cultured and moral in character, the magistrate assigned his men to take the two men to tour the town. They were also permitted to locate a suitable location in the town and build a house in which they would reside in.

While touring the town, they ran into a friend of Michele Ruggieri. Under his advice, they selected a plot of land next to a lake, and began raising funds to build

批准了这项请求，并派人去澳门请罗明坚返回肇庆。

机会难得，罗明坚和利玛窦立即着手准备，于1583年夏末动身前往肇庆。

在肇庆知府衙门，两个外国人按照中国的礼仪向知府行礼，知府也给他们回礼。然后，知府开始询问二人的来历。

罗明坚和利玛窦解释说，他们是侍奉天帝的僧人，因为仰慕泱泱中华帝国的文化，不远万里从遥远的大西洋国渡海而来，希望能在这里找到一处清净的地方，建立圣堂，并且永远留在这片土地上，永不娶妻生子，一心一意终生侍奉天帝。

他们之所以要这样说，是因为明朝政府有规定，外国人如果想定居中国，就不允许再返回故乡，更不能将中国妇女带出国境，否则将受到严惩。当然，他们也不能直接说自己来中国是为了让中国人接受天主教，那样说的后果很可能会是立刻被驱逐出境。

见罗坚明和利玛窦很有诚意，又是有德行的人，知府就吩咐人带他们参观全城，寻找一处合适的地方，允许他们在那里建屋居住。

在参观途中，他们遇上了罗明坚此前在当地认识的

the church. This local friend also invited them to stay at his home till the church was built. The two men were very grateful. When they stepped into the friend's home, they noticed a shrine in the hall, and saw the Chinese characters meaning "Heavenly Father" written on a tablet, they were delighted. During their stay at this friend's house, Michele Ruggieri and Matteo Ricci held mass in this small hall every day, giving thanks to God for His blessings.

Just like that, Michele Ruggieri and Matteo Ricci settled down in Zhaoqing. To them, their progress from Macau to Zhaoqing was a great leap. They felt extremely enthusiastic, knowing that they were one step closer to their Far East dream.

一位朋友。在他的指点下，两人选中了西江边的一处空旷地，准备在此筹建教堂。这位朋友还热情地邀请二人暂时住在他的家里。罗明坚和利玛窦十分感激。他们来到这位朋友家里，看到客厅正中设着祭坛，祭坛上供奉着写有"天主"二字的牌位，更加高兴了。住进去后，他们每天都在这间小厅里举行弥撒，由衷感谢天主赐给他们的一切。

就这样，罗明坚和利玛窦终于在肇庆安定下来。从澳门到肇庆，对于他们来说，无疑是向前迈进了一大步！罗明坚和利玛窦两人眼中放射出热切的光芒：中国，他们的远东梦想，就要一步步地实现了！

Macau and China's Catholicism

In 1553, Portuguese traders gave the excuse of sunning their goods, and began residing in Macau on a long-term basis, settling in Macau's southeastern coast. Following the Portuguese traders, the Catholic missionaries soon arrived in Macau.

In 1556, the Jesuit priest Gregoro Gonzales arrived in Macau, and built the first church. He was followed by the Augustine Council, Dominicans, and Franciscans, who established a presence in Macau, but the most powerful of them were the Jesuits. The Jesuits founded the St. Paul's Theological Seminary in Macau, teaching philosophy, theology, Latin, Chinese, astronomy, mathematics, and Eastern etiquette courses, and specialized in training missionaries were going to preach in China and Japan. At that time, it was the oldest Catholic seminary in China, and was also the largest seminary in the Far East.

In 1576, the Macau diocese was established to take charge of missionary affairs in China, Japan, Korea and Indo-China Peninsula. Macau became the first Catholic missionary center in the Far East. After that, the Catholic movement in Macau developed rapidly, and for a time, churches sprung up all over the city, and there were many Christian converts among the locals. The Jesuits took 35 years building St. Paul's Cathedral, which was the most magnificent church in the Far East.

Due to special geographical location and historical reasons, Macau became the springboard to China mainland in the spread of Catholicism in 16th to 18th century, and therefore became an important intersection of Eastern and Western cultures.

澳门与中国天主教

1553年,葡萄牙商人以"借地晾晒水浸货物"为名,开始在中国东南沿海澳门长期居住。尾随葡萄牙商人来到澳门的,是天主教传教士。

1556年,耶稣会士公匦勒斯(Gregoro Gonzales)来到澳门,建造了澳门第一座教堂。随后奥斯定会、多明我会、方济各会等纷纷在澳门建立据点,其中势力最大者是耶稣会。耶稣会在澳门创办了圣保禄神学院,教授哲学、神学、拉丁文、中文、天文学、数学、东方礼仪等课程,专门培训前往中国内地和日本传教的会士。这是天主教在中国最早的修院,也是当时远东地区最大的修院。

1576年,澳门教区成立,管辖中国、日本、朝鲜及中南半岛各分区的传教事务。澳门成为天主教最早的远东地区传教中心。此后天主教在澳门得到更迅速的发展,一时间教堂林立,教徒甚众。耶稣会耗时35年修建的圣保禄大教堂,是当时远东最宏伟壮观的教堂。

由于特殊的地理位置和历史原因,澳门成为了16—18世纪天主教向中国内地传播的跳板,也因此成为当时中西文化重要的交汇点。

II

The Establishment of the Catholic Movement

Zhaoqing, the first stop into Inner China for Michele Ruggieri and Matteo Ricci, was where the office of the Governor-General of Guangdong and Guangxi was stationed. It was a town that was abundant in natural resources, and was developed in commerce due to its strategic location.

Zhaoqing's magistrate Wang Pan was a local official who was uncorrupted and cared for his people. The people of Zhaoqing were appreciative of his benevolence in governing the town, and had put together money to build him an ancestral hall for him. The plot of land that Matteo Ricci had chosen and was intending to seek for permission, was very near to the Wang Pan's ancestral hall. Wang Pan was an open-minded man, and was not particular on the location of the church. He swiftly approved the application of the Jesuits.

To show their appreciation to Wang Pan, and also to build diplomatic relations with the local government

2

改着儒服，开拓基业

肇庆是当时两广总督府驻地，物产富庶，经济发达，地位重要。这里是罗明坚和利玛窦进入中国内地的第一站。

肇庆知府王泮是位清廉爱民的地方官吏。肇庆百姓感激他的仁政，集资要在西江边为他建造一座生祠（生祠是为活着的人修建祠堂，加以奉祀）。利玛窦他们准备申请修建教堂的那块地，刚好就在为王大人修建的生祠附近。开明的王泮没有多加计较，很快批准了两位外国传教士的申请。

为了报答王大人的美意，也为了将来更好地与肇庆地方官打交道，罗明坚和利玛窦送给他一座自鸣钟。这新奇的洋玩意儿自己能走动，到点就报时，实在是神奇，跟中国传统的计时工具铜壶滴漏完全不同。王泮对它爱不释手，可为了保持自己一贯的清

officials, Michele Ruggieri and Matteo Ricci gave him a chime clock as a present. Wang Pan was fascinated with the clock, which was something new to him. Brought into China from the West, the clock would chime to report time, which was totally different from the traditional time-reporting device of the Chinese. Determined to remain untainted in his career as an honest and uncorrupted magistrate, he returned this expensive and rare gift to the Jesuits. However, he requested the two men to purchase a similar clock on his behalf when they go to Macau, and he would pay for it himself. On top of that, he also allowed them to travel to Macau on board an official boat, in order to help them save on transport expenses.

Michele Ruggieri was then making his way back to Macau to raise funds for the church in Zhaoqing. He swiftly accepted Wang Pan's request, and set off to Macau. Matteo Ricci remained in Zhaoqing to organize the building of the chuch.

At that time, Portugal was engaged in a naval war, and there had not been any trade vessel arriving at the ports of Macau for a long time. Michele Ruggieri was able to obtain a chime clock for Wang Pan. Hence, he decided to hire an India carpenter and build one instead. Then he sent the Indian carpenter to Zhaoqing on board of the official boat, along with all the necessary parts to

廉，还是退还了这昂贵稀罕的礼物。不过，他提出，请罗明坚和利玛窦在澳门帮他代购一座这样的西洋钟，购钟的钱则由他自己来付。他还表示，可以让两位传教士搭乘去往澳门的官船，为他们节省路费。

正打算回澳门为建造教堂募集资金的罗明坚大喜过望，非常爽快地接受了代办的请求，启程前往澳门。利玛窦则留在肇庆，继续天主堂的营建工作。

由于当时葡萄牙正在发动海上战争，已经很久没有新的货船抵达澳门了。罗明坚没法买到自鸣钟，于是他找到一名印度工匠，让工匠带着必要的造钟零件，搭乘王知府的官船先回肇庆。罗明坚将希望寄托在印度工匠和学过自鸣钟制造的利玛窦身上，希望他们能在肇庆当地造出王大人想要的西洋

肇庆崇禧塔，1582年由肇庆知府王泮主持修建。利玛窦和罗明坚修建的天主堂即在崇禧塔旁。
Chongxi Pagoda in Zhaoqing, commissioned by Zhaoqing's magistrate Wang Pan, completed in 1582. Xianhua Temple was sited next to Chongxi Pagoda.

put together the chime clock. Michele Ruggieri put all his hopes on the Indian carpenter and Matteo Ricci, who had learnt how to make a chime clock. He hoped that the two men would be able to produce the clock that Wang Pan wanted.

In Zhaoqing, Matteo Ricci managed to build the first level of the church. He owed this to the assistance of some kind gentlemen of Zhaoqing, who were friendly to foreigners, and had donated generously to their cause. For a while, the church had not included any form of Western decorations, and was similar to the local buildings in its architecture. Because of that, it did not invite any negative comments from the local people.

When the Indian carpenter arrived in Zhaoqing, Matteo Ricci immediately understood Michele Ruggieri's intention. He went personally to the magistrate's office and informed Wang Pan of their plan. Wang Pan was very understanding and did not mind it at all. With that, Matteo Ricci began

利玛窦在中国制造的自鸣钟（复制品）
The chime clock made by Matteo Ricci in China. (Replica.)

钟来。

留在肇庆的利玛窦已经想方设法把天主堂的第一层盖了起来。他得到了当地一些对外国人友善的绅士的资助。这座洋建筑暂时还没有加上西式装饰，和中国本土建筑相比，差别并不是很大，因而没有引起当地人太多的非议。

印度工匠一抵达肇庆，利玛窦就领会了罗明坚的意图。他亲自去官衙告诉王知府他们的计划，取得了这位通情达理的大人的谅解，然后开始着手研制中国第一座本土生产的自鸣钟。

附近的居民看到两个外国人成天在那儿敲敲打打，十分好奇，不懂事的小孩子还经常恶作剧地往天主堂里扔石头。一天，印度工匠正在埋头磨制自鸣钟要用到的一个小轴承时，被小孩子投掷的石头砸中了。他很生气，立刻跑出去，抓住了淘气的孩子。为了吓唬这些孩子，让他们以后不再捣乱，工匠将其中为首的一个关在一间小屋里。

利玛窦知道了这个消息，赶紧让工匠放掉孩子，以免招来当地居民的不满。可在一些人的怂恿下，那孩子家里一个游手好闲的远方亲戚还是上官府报了

the research and making of the first chime clock ever made in China.

The residents living near the church was curious to see the two men busy constructing the clock. Mischievous children frequently threw stones at the church. Once, when the Indian carpenter was busy making a bearing for the clock, a stone cast by one of the children hit him on the head. He was furious and ran out of the church and caught hold of the children. In order to intimidate the children so that they would not play prank on him, the carpenter locked one of children into a hut.

When Matteo Ricci got wind of it, he urged the carpenter to immediately release the child, in order not to provoke the residents. However, under the persuasion of some people, the relatives of the child make a report to the magistrate's office, accusing Matteo Ricci and the carpenter of abducting and trafficking children.

Wang Pan knew Matteo Ricci well, and believed that he was a righteous man, but he had no evidence to prove his innocence. In order to protect Matteo Ricci, so as to appease the angry crowd, Wang Pan put all the blames on the carpenter, and ordered him to leave Zhaoqing. Fortunately, some righteous residents stood up for him, testifying that the two foreigners were law-abiding people, and had engaged in any criminal activity or abducted children for trafficking. The whistleblowers

穿儒服的传教士

案，诬告利玛窦他们拐卖人口。

知府王泮十分清楚利玛窦的为人，但苦于缺乏有力的证据。为了保护利玛窦，又能对民众有所交代，王大人只好判决所有的过错都在于印度工匠，限令他立刻离开肇庆。幸运的是，一些正义的居民此时挺身而出，作证说这两个外国人一向安分守己，并没有做过犯法的事，更没有拐卖人口。告发者自知无理，只得承认是诬陷。利玛窦他们没有受到这起官司的影响，继续在肇庆研究怎样制造自鸣钟。

利玛窦和印度工匠费了很多功夫，终于完成了任务，将一座崭新的自鸣钟送进王大人的住处。这珍贵的礼物让王大人十分高兴，小心地把它安放在府衙里。不过，由于手下没有人会给这宝贝自鸣钟上发条，总是麻烦利玛窦他们进府调试也不方便，后来王大人又把它送还给了利玛窦。

利玛窦和罗明坚修建的中国历史上第一座天主教堂"仙花寺"遗址

The historic site of Xianhua Temple, the first Catholic church in China, built by Matteo Ricci and Michele Ruggieri.

knew that they did not have a case, and admitted that it was all made up. Matteo Ricci was not affected by the case, and continued to study how he could construct the clock.

After much effort by Matteo Ricci and the carpenter, the task was finally accomplished. The two men sent a brand new chime clock to the residence of Wang Pan. Wang Pan was delighted to receive this gift, and placed it in his office. However, as none of his men knew how to wind the clock, they found it cumbersome to ask Matteo Ricci to come to the office to get it done all the time. Hence, Wang Pan sent the clock back to Matteo Ricci.

The money that Michele Ruggieri raised in Macau contributed greatly to the building of the church. The church had now two levels, instead of one. The chime clock that was placed in the church was also a rare treasure that was not often seen in any ordinary buildings. Standing beside the West Lake, the European style architecture soon became a place of interest in Zhaoqing, attracting many sightseers from around the area.

Out of his friendship with Matteo Ricci, Wang Pan named the church Xianhua Temple, and personally inscribed the church's inscribed board, which he delivered to Matteo Ricci in a loud procession. This

肇庆城北郊七星岩风景区。王泮任肇庆知府期间，开始对这里的原始山水进行开发，建成远近闻名的风景名胜。
Seven Star Crags Scenic Area, northern suburb of Zhaoqing City.

　　这时，罗明坚从澳门带回的资金已经有效地发挥了作用，原先一层的天主堂被增修为两层。矗立在西江边的这座欧式建筑，迅速成为肇庆的一处名胜，吸引了很多当地甚至临近地区的人前去参观。

　　出于和利玛窦的友好关系，王泮为天主堂命名"仙花寺"，并亲自撰写了匾额，又派人敲锣打鼓地将匾额送到利玛窦的住处。这一举动让当地居民明白，这个洋人和他修的房子受到地方长官的保护。从此，再也没有人敢做破坏的事了。

　　从和王泮的交往中，利玛窦第一次深切体会到，

Missionary in Confucian Garb

move showed the local residents that this foreigner and his building were both under the protection of the magistrate. From then on, no one dared to sabotage Matteo Ricci.

From his interaction with Wang Pan, Matteo Ricci profoundly understood that to begin a smooth course in missionary work, one must assimilate into the high society and forge good relations with the officials who had power to make decisions. This became the strategy employed by the Jesuit all around the world.

Between 1583 and 1600, Matteo Ricci visited several cities in the south of China, including Guangzhou, Zhaoqing, Shaozhou, Nanchang, and Nanjing. Initially, Matteo Ricci wanted to side with Buddhism in his mission work. He understood that Buddhism, which first came to China during the Han Dynasty (206 BC–220 AD), had gone through a long process of development, and had become a Chinese religion. Being a deeply entrenched part of the Chinese's spiritual life, it would not be easily replaced by another foreign religion. Therefore, he wanted to reach out to the Chinese people as Western monks, so as to be readily accepted by them, which he believed would greatly help in his missionary work. The name bestowed by Wang Pan for his church also resembled the name of a Buddhist monastery, which aided in creating a deeper understanding of its purpose.

在中国，要想顺利传教，首先就要进入上流社会，和掌握权力的官员搞好关系。这也是他所在的耶稣会在世界各地传教时采取的一贯策略。

1583—1600年间，利玛窦先后到过中国南方的广州、肇庆、韶州、南昌、南京等地。

最初，利玛窦想向佛教靠拢。他了解到，印度佛教从汉代（前206—公元220）传入中国，经过长期的发展，早已成为一种完全"中国化"的宗教，不再被当作外来宗教而受排斥，反而成为中国人精神生活的一部分。因此，他希望中国人把他们这些传教士看成是来自西方的和尚，这样也许能够更快地被中国人接受，有利于传教工作的展开。肇庆知府王泮将他们的天主堂命名为"仙花寺"，其实也是佛教寺庙的名字。于是，利玛窦剃掉了头发和胡须，脱下自己的教服，改穿和尚的僧袍。

直到利玛窦遇到瞿太素——一位对西方科学深感兴趣，偏偏不想通过科举考试做官的有名儒士，他才从这位贵族公子那里了解到，原来和尚在中国的社会地位并不高，一些修养不够的和尚甚至为非作歹、触犯法律，导致整个僧侣阶层的名声都受到影响。利玛

Hence, Matteo Ricci shaved off his hair and beard, discarded his Jesuit's outfit, and put on a monk's robe.

He carried on with this for a while, until he met Qu Taisu, a well-known Confucian scholar who had a keen interest in the Western science, and had resisted obtaining an official position through sitting for the imperial examination. From Qu Taisu, he realized that the social status of the monks were not as high as he thought, and some monks were even engaged in unlawful activities, affecting the reputation of the monks in general. Matteo Ricci then came to the realization that the most respected people in China's society were the scholars, just like Qu Taisu. The scholars were not only educated and knowledgeable, but they were also court officials, who were selected for excelling in the imperial examination. As such, they were directly influencing the nation's development.

Enlightened, Matteo Ricci discarded his monk's robe, and put on the attire of a Confucian scholar. He wanted to present himself as an educated, moral and cultured man, just like the Chinese Confucian scholars.

Through Qu Taisu, Matteo Ricci got to know many Confucian scholars. Interacting with them significantly enhanced his understanding of Chinese culture. He felt that China was unique in many aspects, such as the achievements made in the area of medicine,

身着中国儒服的利玛窦
Matteo Ricci dressed in Chinese Confucian garb.

窦终于明白，在中国，最受人尊敬的其实是瞿太素这样的读书人，他们不但有学问，而且可以通过科举考试成为朝廷官员、社会中坚，对整个国家产生影响。

　　醒悟后的利玛窦马上脱下了僧袍，换上和瞿太素一样的儒士服装，以此表示自己和那些穿同样衣服的中国人一样，有学问、有道德、有修养。

mathematics, and astronomy, etc. He also found that scientific development in China was more advanced that the West, but to the Chinese, it was an endeavor that did not deserve too much effort and attention.

To many local people, Matteo Ricci and other missionaries were mysterious people. They suspected that they were alchemists, as they did not work and yet have an endless supply of money—they did not know that the money was offerings from Macau. The fair complexion of Matteo Ricci, which looked pink, was shocking to some of the locals, who thought that he had found an elixir to immortality, and not knowing that the skin color of Europeans were naturally different from the Asians.

Many Confucian scholars were amazed and admired the knowledge in Western science that Matteo Ricci shared with them. Matteo Ricci shared with them all that he had learnt in astronomy, mathematics, physics, chemistry, languages and logic. He also showed them the equipment and apparatus used in astronomy that he brought to China with him. They included the telescope, the sundial, astrolabe, and prisms, etc. Such "incredible tales" and "strange equipment" that they had only heard of were unraveled to these scholars. They were very impressed by what they saw and were full of admiration for Matteo Ricci. Within a short period of time, the

通过瞿太素，利玛窦结识了更多的文人儒士。与他们的交往使利玛窦对中国文化有了更加深入的了解。他认为中国在很多方面是举世无双的，中国人在医学、数学、天文学等领域的知识都非常丰富。同时他也发现，尽管中国的科学研究已经比较发达，但中国人往往认为科学研究并不重要，不值得为此投入太多精力。

而在很多当地人眼中，利玛窦以及他的传教士伙伴仍然显得有些神秘莫测。一些人认为，传教士不用亲自劳动，却总有用不完的钱，一定是懂得炼金的法术——他们不知道传教士经常接受来自澳门的布施。利玛窦等人白里透红的肤色，也令一些人惊异，认为这是因为掌握了长生不老的秘方——他们不知道欧洲人的肤色与亚洲人天生就不同。

也有很多儒士对利玛窦所介绍的西方科学知识感到好奇和仰慕。利玛窦给他们讲解自己来中国前所学的天文历法、数学、物理、化学，还有语言、逻辑等知识，又向他们展示自己从西方带来的各种天文仪器、机械物品，比如西洋镜、日晷、星盘、三棱镜等。这些前所未闻的"奇谈"和从未见过的"奇

reputation of the knowledgeable Matteo Ricci spread far and wide.

In Zhaoqing, Matteo Ricci created five of the many "firsts" of China. Other than the first Catholic church that he built, and the first chime clock that he constructed, he also established the first library of foreign books, illustrated the first atlas in China, and wrote the first English dictionary in China.

Matteo Ricci arranged all the books he brought with him in order and placed them in a room in his residence for his visitors to read. The collection of books included *The Holy Bible* and Euclid's *Elements*. It became the first library of foreign books in China. Later, Matteo Ricci wrote to the Jesuits in Europe, and requested for more books to be sent to Zhaoqing, so as to help him expand the library and attract more readers. In this library hung an oil painting of Virgin Mary and the Infant Jesus, which resembled a portrait of the Goddess of Mercy (a Buddhist Bodhisattva) Bestows Babies. Because of this close resemblance, many people came to pray and offer incense to the painting. This caused Matteo Ricci a considerable amount of worry that the Chinese people would mix up God in Catholicism with a Buddhist deity. Worst of all, they might wrongly perceive the god of Catholicism as female. So he took the painting of Mother Mary and Baby Jesus off the wall, and put up a portrait

穿儒服的传教士

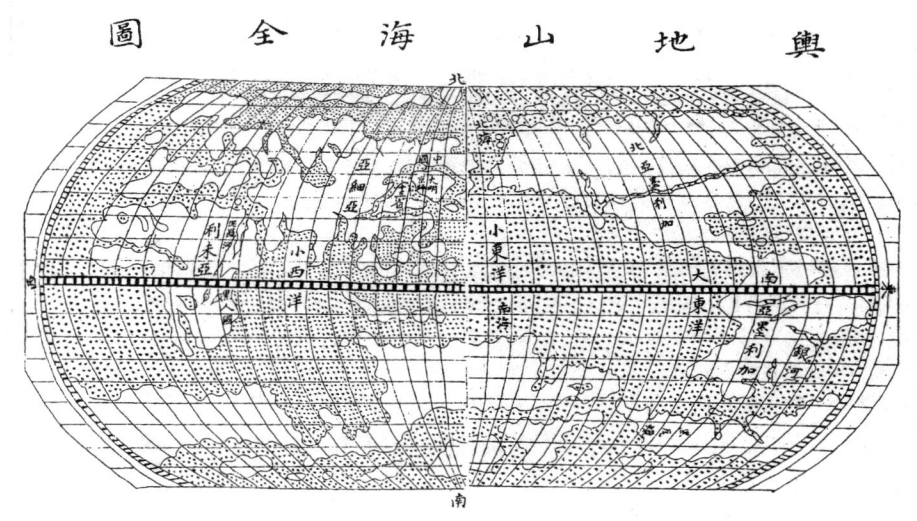

圖　全　海　山　地　輿

利玛窦《舆地山海全图》。在肇庆时，到利玛窦房间去的中国文人们最喜欢的东西之一，就是挂在墙上的这幅世界地图。
Matteo Ricci's world map. In Zhaoqing, one of the items in Matteo Ricci's room that many people enjoyed admiring was this world map that hung on the wall.

器"，使儒士们大开眼界，对利玛窦十分钦佩。一时间，利玛窦博学的美名四处传扬。

在肇庆，利玛窦创造了中国历史上的五个第一——除了前文提到的建造了中国内地第一座天主教堂、研制出中国本土第一座自鸣钟之外，他还建立了中国第一家外文书图书馆，绘制了中国第一幅世界地图，编写出中国第一本西文字典。

利玛窦将带来的《圣经》和欧几里德《几何原本》等西方书籍整理好，放在住所的一个房间里，供

of Jesus Christ instead. However, he avoided displaying a painting of the Passion of Jesus, as he deemed it too bloody and violent to be acceptable by the Chinese.

Many visitors were amazed by the world map that Matteo Ricci had brought to China. It was the first time they were introduced to the Westerners' study of geography. Matteo Ricci also illustrated the first world map in the Chinese language. In order to suit the interest of the intellectual Chinese, he shifted the prime meridian such that China became the center of the world. This certainly helped in satisfying the perception of China as the middle kingdom, and the Chinese people would be more inclined to find out what the world beyond China was like, such as the customs and traditions of other countries. For instance, when Wang Pan saw that the world was so vast besides China, and that there were so many countries, he found it unbelievable. He found even it even more incredible when Matteo Ricci told him that the Earth is round. For generations, all the Chinese, like him, had been taught that the sky was round and the earth equilateral. It was something that many like him had never doubted their forebears. His perception of the world was China, and some islands that surrounded it. Deeply affected by it, he came out with some money and printed several copies of the map and gave them to his friends as gifts. The map was reprinted many times

人参观。这里便成为了中国第一家外文书图书馆。后来利玛窦还写信回欧洲，要求寄更多的书籍来肇庆，帮助他扩大图书馆，吸引更多人的兴趣。这间图书馆里还悬挂有圣母玛利亚怀抱圣婴的画像，因为酷似中国的送子观音图，引得许多当地人纷纷前来跪拜、焚香祷告。利玛窦担心中国人会因而将天主教上帝和他们的佛教神灵混淆，或者误认为天主教的唯一真神是女性，又改挂了一幅基督像。不过，为了使中国人容易接受，他并没有将基督受难那血淋淋的场景展示出来。

利玛窦带来的世界地图，特别令参观者们惊讶，因为这是他们第一次接触到西方近代地理学知识。利玛窦还亲自绘制出中国第一幅世界地图——《山海舆地全图》。为了迎合中国知识分子，他巧妙地移动了本初子午线，让中国处于整个世界的中心。这样，中国人"天朝上国"的心理得到了满足，也就很愿意进一步看看他们之外的世界是什么样子，甚至还会向利玛窦询问其他国家的风俗礼仪。就拿肇庆知府王泮来说，当在地图上看到除了中国外，世界还那么辽阔，还分布着那么多别的国家，他简直无法相信自己的眼

Missionary in Confucian Garb

around the world, and many people pride themselves for owning a copy of it.

In order to help more Jesuit missionaries learn Chinese, Matteo Ricci and Michele Ruggieri co-edited the first Western dictionary in China, *The Portuguese-Chinese Dictionary*. Their decision to select Portuguese was due to the fact that many missionaries who came to China were Portuguese, and the missions were mainly sponsored by Portuguese traders. The dictionary would help many of them in picking up the Chinese language.

Matteo Ricci and Michele Ruggieri had not once forgotten their mission as Jesuit priests. All the education

罗明坚《中国地图集》封面。罗明坚返回欧洲期间，出版了西方第一部详细的中国地图集。
The cover of Michele Ruggieri's *Atlas of China*. This was the first comprehensive Western atlas of China that was published by Michele Ruggieri upon his return to Europe.

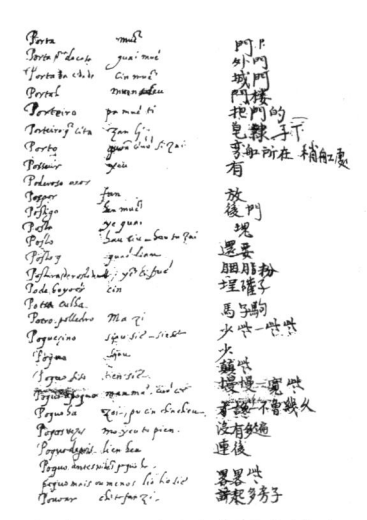

利玛窦、罗明坚合编的《葡华辞典》残页
The torn pages of the *Portuguese-Chinese Dictionary*, edited by Michele Ruggieri and Matteo Ricci.

睛。后来利玛窦再告诉他地球是圆的时，他更是觉得不可思议。从小他就被教导说天是圆的、地是方的，在他的脑海中，世界的概念就是中国再加上周围的一些岛屿。其实不仅是他，几千年来几乎所有的中国人都接受着同样的知识，并且深信他们前辈的观点。王泮深受震撼，他自己出钱刊印这幅地图，作为礼物送给朋友。这幅地图后来被翻刻达12次之多，流传到中国各地，很多中国知识分子都以拥有《山海舆地全图》为荣。

为了帮助更多的传教士能够进入中国传教，利玛窦和罗明坚一起编纂了中国第一部西文字典——《葡华辞典》。因为当时很多到中国来的传教士是葡萄牙人，传教的经费也主要来自在澳门的葡萄牙商人，所以他们选择了使用葡萄牙语，希望更多人能够借助这部字典学会中文。

身为耶稣会士，利玛窦和罗明坚一刻也没有忘记自己的传教使命。展示各种新奇的事物，介绍西方的科学

that started in various aspects of Western science, was aimed at instilling an interest among the Chinese people. Using that as a platform, they could then proceed to spreading the Catholic faith to them. Together, they translated *The Ten Commandments*, *The Lord's Prayer*, *Our Lady of Hymn*, and *Catechism*. Michele Ruggieri also published a Chinese catechism. These books were given to the Chinese who were interested in the Catholic faith. However, Matteo Ricci acknowledged that at that time, many Chinese were not well informed of Catholicism. Yet, he insisted on seizing any opportunity he had to interact with the intellectual Chinese, and the government officials, in order to preach to them.

In 1588, Michele Ruggieri returned to Roma, and requested the Pope to formally dispatch envoys to China. The matter was not attended to as four of the Popes passed away consecutively. Not too long after, Michele Ruggieri passed away in his hometown. He had left behind the China that he had once contributed great effort in his missionary work. Matteo Ricci, who was still in China, had to take over a far more important role to complete his mission. Yet, for him, what was more important then was to build good relations on the societal level.

知识，主要目的都是为了吸引中国人的兴趣，从而可以进一步向中国人宣传天主教信仰。他们翻译了《祖传天主十诫》、《主的祈祷》、《圣母赞歌》和《教理问答书》，罗明坚又用中文编写了《天主实录》。一旦发现有中国人流露出对天主教的兴趣，他们就会向其派发这些书籍。不过，利玛窦自己也承认，当时大多数中国人对于天主教并没有什么深刻的认识。但他还是坚持抓住每一次与中国文人、官僚交流的机会，努力将自己的宗教信仰完整地传达给他们。

1588年，罗明坚返回罗马，请求教皇派遣正式使节到中国。当时正好赶上连续四位教皇先后"升天"，教廷向中国派遣特使的事被搁置下来。不久罗明坚因病在家乡去世，没能再回到他付出心血开拓传教事业的中国。留在中国的利玛窦从此必须承担更大的责任，完成更多的工作。而他的当务之急，还是尽可能广泛地在中国建立社会关系。

The Jesuits in the 16th Century

In 1540, the Pope gave the formal approval to the Spanish nobility Ignacio de Loyola to form the order of Jesuits. The Jesuits' headquarters was located in Rome, and its founder's mission was to fight the "heretical" Protestants, maintain the authority of the Catholic Church and the Pope, and convert the infidels around the world to Christianity. The Jesuits would be dispatched all over the world and preach to people from all walks of life.

The Jesuits placed their emphasis on education, and only recruited young men aged 16–18. At first, the Jesuits were educated in Latin, followed later by theology, literature and other humanities and natural science subjects, so as to impart religious and moral training, and knowledge together in their missionary work. From the late 16th century, higher education in the Catholic regions of Europe was almost entirely monopolized by the Jesuits. The Jesuits paid particular attention to the cultivation of the children of high society, so that they could exercise their influence as Jesuits in the high society around the world. Matteo Ricci was an outstanding representative of this elite education.

16世纪的耶稣会

1540年，罗马教皇正式批准西班牙贵族伊纳爵·罗耀拉（Ignacio de Loyola）创立耶稣会。耶稣会总部设在罗马，其创立的宗旨就是同"异端"新教作斗争，维护天主教会和教皇的权威，使全世界异教徒都能皈依基督。他们派遣会士深入世界各地，在社会各阶层中广泛传道。

耶稣会重视教育，规定只招收16—18岁的青年男子入会。起初主要让他们学习拉丁文，随后再开设神学、文学等人文学科和各门自然科学课程，将宗教道德训练和知识传授结合在一起，用知识为传教服务。从16世纪后期起，欧洲天主教地区的高等教育几乎全部被耶稣会所垄断。耶稣会尤其注重对上流社会子弟的培养，以便将来他们能以耶稣会士身份，进入世界各国的上流社会发挥作用。利玛窦正是这种精英教育的杰出代表。

III

The Long-awaited Entrance to Beijing

In the summer of 1589, the Governor-General of Guangzhou and Guangxi was replaced again. This newly appointed Governor-General, Liu Jiezhai, was not as friendly as his predecessors. The first thing he did was to confiscate Xianhua Temple and convert it into his official residence. However, Matteo Ricci was clever in employing the use of diplomacy to negotiate for another place in which he could settle in. Upon getting the approval to relocate to Shaozhou, another city in Guangzhou, Matteo Ricci left Zhaoqing and a congregation of 80 converts.

Shaozhou was unlike Zhaoqing, which had friendly government officials such as Wang Pan who could offer him protection. Matteo Ricci's life in Shaozhou was therefore not as pleasant as that in Zhaoqing. In order to avoid too much unnecessary attention, Matteo Ricci built his church using entirely Chinese architectural style. Despite his effort, troubles still came knocking on his

3

辗转反复，终入皇城

　　1589年夏天，两广总督又换人了。新上任的总督刘节斋不像他的两位前任那样友好，下令将仙花寺收归公有，作为总督官邸。聪明的利玛窦虽然不得不离开肇庆和那里的80名教友，却运用外交手段使刘总督作出妥协，允许他前往广东的另一座城市韶州，并在那里定居。

　　移居韶州，没有王泮那样友善、开放的官员提供保护，利玛窦的日子没有从前好过。为了避免太引人注目，他在韶州修建的天主堂采用了中式建筑风格。尽管利玛窦尽量低调，可麻烦还是找上了他。

　　1592年的一天夜里，一群醉酒的人拿着斧头等武器，涌进他的住所大吵大闹。利玛窦在躲避的过程中，不慎摔伤了腿。虽然后来歹徒被捉拿归案，但腿伤却跟随了他好一阵子。不过，中国政府在处理这起

door.

One particular night in 1592, a group of drunkards charged into his house brandishing weapons such as axes, creating a ruckus. During the skirmish, Matteo Ricci fell and injured his leg. Even though the culprits were apprehended by the authority, Matteo Ricci had to deal with the injury for a long period of time. Still, he felt thankful and moved by the justice that was dealt by the Chinese government in dealing with the case. Despite his plea for clemency on behalf of the convicts, they were still severely dealt with in the end.

What saddened him, after Michele Ruggieri had returned to Europe, was the passing of two Jesuit priests who were with him – Antoine de Mello and Francois de Petris. His only consolation came in 1594, when the Jesuits sent him an assistant Lazzaro Cattaneo, to help him in his mission. At the same time, through his relations with Qu Taisu, Matteo Ricci gradually gained acceptance among the scholars and officials of Shaozhou.

In 1595, Matteo Ricci finally achieved a breakthrough, which offered him a long-awaited opportunity. That year, the assistant minister of the Ministry of War—Shi Xing—was summoned to Beijing. Before Shi Xing departed from Shaozhou, he requested Matteo Ricci to teach his son methods to enhance his memory skill. Shi Xing's son had failed his last imperial examination and had to begin

利玛窦的地图被多次刻印，图为冯应京《月令广义》收入的《山海舆地全图》。
Matteo Ricci's map was reprinted many times. The picture shows Matteo Ricci's world map included in Feng Yingjing's *Yue Ling Guang Yi*.

案件时的公正态度，令利玛窦感到欣慰。尽管利玛窦本人也为罪犯求情，地方官员还是对这些人进行了严惩。

让他难过的是，在罗明坚返回欧洲后，陪伴在自己身边的两名耶稣会士——麦安东（Antoine de Mello）和石方西（Francois de Petris）相继去世。还好，1594年，教会又派来郭居静（Lazzaro Cattaneo）协助他的工作。同时，通过瞿太素的关系，韶州的文人和官员也渐渐接受了他。

这时，一次新的机遇悄悄来临了。

1595年，兵部侍郎石星奉万历皇帝（1573—1619在位）旨意，要乘船从韶州去北京。石星请求利玛窦陪伴他儿子一段时间，传授一些记忆的方

preparing for his next one. Matteo Ricci was delighted as this could be a chance for him to go to Beijing, a long-time wish of his.

On their way to Beijing, the boat met with a mishap. No only that many important luggage were lost, one young priest, who was a good swimmer, was drowned. Fortunately, Matteo Ricci, who did not know how to swim, was rescued from the river.

However, in 1592, Japan waged a war against Korea, which was a vassal state of China. The Ming government, at the request of the Korean king, sent an army to take on the Japanese. Due to this war, the political atmosphere in Beijing was very intense, and being a foreigner, Matteo Ricci had not even a slim chance in entering China's capital. Disappointed, he decided to stay in Nanjing for the time being.

In Nanjing, Matteo Ricci met with some long-time friends, who hosted receptions for him. At these functions, Matteo Ricci befriended many high-society people. The Chinese had the habit of inviting one another to their social functions, hence Matteo Ricci was always invited. Through all these social functions, Matteo Ricci befriended more people, and gradually expand his social circle in Nanjing.

In the summer of 1595, Matteo Ricci set off to Nanchang. The road from Nanjing to Nanchang was another great

法，因为他儿子刚在科举考试中失败，需要尽早准备下一次的考试。利玛窦大喜过望，如果能够借此机会进入北京，那真是再好也不过的事情！

路途上，他们的船只发生了意外，不仅丢失了很多重要的行李，还淹死了一名水性很好的年轻教士。万幸的是，不谙水性的利玛窦虽然也落水，却被救了上来。

然而，由于1592年日本发动战争，企图吞并当时中国的属国朝鲜，应朝鲜国王请求，明朝出兵援朝，正在对日作战，北京的政治气氛非常紧张。作为一个外国人，利玛窦根本没有办法在这样的时刻进入中国的首都，他只好沮丧地决定先在南京逗留。

在南京，利玛窦遇到一位从前的朋友，受到了热情的款待。在这位朋友举办的宴席上，他又新结交了许多有身份的中国人。中国人之间经常互相回请，每次的宴席都会给利玛窦送去请帖。这样利玛窦结识的人越来越多，在南京的交际圈渐渐扩大。

1595年夏天，利玛窦又启程前往南昌。从南京到南昌，是一次重要的跨越——南昌众多的学者和前来赶考的文人，让利玛窦找到了通过知识传教的最佳对

leap for Matteo Ricci. Nanchang was an examination center and attracted many scholars and educated people to it. It was an ideal place for Matteo Ricci, as these people became the audience to which Matteo Ricci could minister to through the transmission of knowledge to them. He felt himself getting closer to the intellectual people in China.

Matteo Ricci lived in Nanchang for three years, and it left with him a very good impression. There were a number of well-known education institutions in Nanchang, and many scholars and educated Chinese congregate in the city. The streets of Nanchang were preceded by beautifully crafted memorial arch, which recorded the names of the scholars who had succeeded in the examination and appointed as government officials. Knowledge was revered in the city, which was bathed in a rich atmosphere of knowledge seeking. Matteo Ricci was full of praise for the city. During his stay there, he was given the chance to observe the imperial examination held in Jiangxi, and he laboriously recorded every detail of the examination, and introduced the system to Europe, which attracted much praise from the European community.

In Nanchang, Matteo Ricci completely altered his methods in preaching. He did not build a single church there, neither did he openly preach to the people. Instead, he diverted all his energy to befriending the educated Chinese. During a personal conversation or discussion,

穿儒服的传教士

广州怀圣寺，是中国最早创建的清真寺之一。据说利玛窦在广州时，曾运用几何原理，目测出寺中塔的高度，令在座的中国官员、文人惊叹不已。
Huaisheng Temple in Guangzhou, one of China's earliest mosques. Legend had it that when Matteo Ricci was in Guangzhou, he used geometric principles to estimate the height of a pagoda in the temple, to the amazement of the Chinese officials that were present.

象。他和中国知识界的距离更近了。

利玛窦在南昌住了三年，这里给他留下了非常美好的印象。久负盛名的白鹿洞书院就在南昌附近，所以南昌总是聚集着很多知名学者和向往知识的年轻人。南昌街头比比皆是雕刻精美的牌坊，记录着当地通过科举考试成功做官、为家族光宗耀祖的名人事迹。浓郁的知识氛围和对知识的尊重，让利玛窦赞不绝口。其间，他还有幸目睹了一次江西科举乡试的盛况。利玛窦费了很多笔墨将考试的种种细节记录下来，介绍到欧洲去，引起了当时欧洲人对中国选官制度的钦羡。

到南昌后，利玛窦彻底改变了自己的传教方式。

and when an opportunity arose, he would share the gospels with them.

The knowledgeable and humble Matteo Ricci won the hearts of many educated Chinese, who regarded him as one of their own. Very quickly, he became a prominent man in the city of Nanchang. On 22 September 1596, he successfully predicted a solar eclipse, which catapulted him to greater fame. He made fast friends with many distinguished Chinese, including Prince Jian An.

In 1597, his superior Alessandro Valignano appointed Matteo Ricci as the the Major Superior of the Jesuits' mission in China, and was left fully in charge of the mission work in China. He instructed Matteo Ricci to try to seek an audience with the Chinese emperor, in order to speed up the process of the mission work in China. The newly appointed Matteo Ricci thus began planning his trip to Beijing.

Later, Matteo Ricci got hold of the information that his friend Wang Honghai was going to Nanjing to take up the position of the Minister of the Board of Rites. He immediately requested that Wang Honghai take him along to Nanjing, where he would try to make his way to Beijing. Wang agreed swiftly, and told Matteo Ricci that he would take him to Beijing to attend the birthday celebration of the emperor.

In June 1598, Matteo Ricci, along with Guo Jujing and

江西庐山白鹿洞书院。利玛窦在南昌期间，与白鹿洞书院院长章潢及其门人子弟来往密切。
Bailudong Academy, Lushan Mountain, Jiangxi. During his stay in Nanchang, Matteo Ricci socialized frequently with the principal of Bailudong Academy Zhang Huang and his students.

他没有修建教堂，也不公开向中国百姓宣讲天主教教义，而是把所有精力都放在结交中国知识分子上。在私下间的谈话、讨论中，利玛窦会择机向他们传播福音。

博学而谦逊的利玛窦赢得了众多中国文人的好感，他几乎被他们当作是自己群体中的一员。利玛窦很快就成为南昌城里的一位名人。1596年9月22日，利

Wang Honghai, departed Nanchang to Nanjing. They brought along many gifts from Macau to present to the Chinese emperor as birthday presents. A month later, they arrived in Nanjing, and in September, arrived in Tongzhou, which was very near to Beijing.

Unfortunately, Japan was invading Korea, and Beijing was heavily guarded. Hence, Matteo Ricci did not manage to obtain the authorization to enter Beijing. Disappointed, he made his way back to Nanjing. Along the way, he suddenly fell ill in Suzhou, but was lucky to have Qu Taisu, who happened to be in Suzhou at that time, nursing him back to health. In February 1599, Matteo Ricci returned to Nanjing

This time round, Matteo Ricci decided to remain in Nanjing, so that he could seize the right opportunity to return to Beijing. He spent the Spring Festival of 1599 at the residence of Wang Honghai. The Spring Festival was a time of reunion in a family, and having just recovered from a serious illness, Matteo Ricci began to miss home. He yearned to seek an audience with the Chinese emperor as soon as he could, so that he could accomplish his mission. With the help of Wang Honghai, he purchased a house in Nanjing, and began his long wait. On ordinary days, he continued to socialize with the intellectual Chinese and tried to widen his circle of influence. At the same time, he tried his utmost to continue preaching the

玛窦成功预测到一次日食。这使他在当地越发出名，并结交了更多权贵，受到明朝皇室建安王等贵族的热情款待。

1597年，范礼安任命利玛窦为耶稣会中国教区会长，全权负责在中国的传教活动，并指示利玛窦设法进京觐见中国皇帝，以达到在整个中国迅速展开传教工作的目的。接受了新任务的利玛窦开始再次策划北京之行。

不久，利玛窦得到消息，他的朋友王弘诲将去南京担任礼部尚书。利玛窦马上请求王弘诲带他同行，希望能先到南京，再设法去北京。王弘诲不仅爽快地答应了，还表示要带利玛窦去北京，一同参加万历皇帝的生日庆典。

1598年6月，利玛窦、郭居静同王弘诲一起离开南昌。他们随身携带了许多从澳门送来准备献给中国皇帝的礼物。7月，他们到达南京，9月，抵达北京附近的通州。

不巧的是，这次又遇上日本侵犯朝鲜，京城戒备森严，利玛窦没有获得入京许可。无奈的他只好再度折返。

Missionary in Confucian Garb

gospel and to educate the people on Western knowledge.

Nanjing was the former capital of the Ming Dynasty. Although the capital was moved to Beijing, Nanjing pretty much retained most of the governing systems and grandeur that was similar to Beijing. To familiarize himself with Nanjing would no doubt facilitate Matteo Ricci's mission work in Beijing in future. Hence, he began to make close observations of Nanjing. In the process of which, he was greatly impressed by its architecture, temples, pagodas and bridges, as well as the talented and well-mannered people, the rich and abundant land and the beautiful scenery of the countryside. He hailed Nanjing as the leading city in the whole of China and the Orient. He familiarized himself with governmental organizations of Nanjing, so as to prepare for his eventual advancement to Beijing. Even though he did not know when that day would be, he was enthusiastic and determined that one day, he would be summoned by the emperor to Beijing. Then, with the influence of the emperor, he would be able to spread the gospels to the Chinese people and convert them to Christianity.

Matteo Ricci did not wait too long for that day. A year later, he got the opportunity to go to Beijing again. His friend Zhu Shilu helped him to prepare the necessary documents, and arranged for him to travel to Beijing on board a boat carrying tributes to Beijing. By then, Matteo

17世纪欧洲人笔下的南京城街道。利玛窦曾说，论秀丽和雄伟，南京超过世界上所有城市。
17th-century Europeans' impression of Nanjing's streets. Matteo Ricci once said Nanjing's beauty and majesty surpassed all the cities in the world.

  路过苏州时，利玛窦突染重病，幸亏有正在苏州的瞿太素照顾，他才逐渐康复。1599年2月，利玛窦回到南京。

  这次利玛窦决定留在南京，以便随时抓住机遇，重新向北京进发。他在王弘诲的府邸度过了1599年的元宵节。这个中国人阖家团圆的日子，让孤身在外多年又大病初愈的利玛窦有些思乡心切，也让他更加渴望能早日见到中国皇帝，完成自己肩负的使命。在王

Missionary in Confucian Garb

17世纪欧洲人笔下的南京报恩寺琉璃塔。利玛窦对南京的宫殿、庙宇、塔、桥十分赞赏，称欧洲没有能超过它们的类似建筑。
17th-century Europeans' impression of the glass pagoda in Nanjing's Bao'en Temple. Matteo Ricci was an admirer of Nanjing's palace, temples, towers, and bridges, saying that Europe had no similar architecture that could match them.

Ricci would have persevered for this day for 19 years. This time, he was determined to seek an audience with the emperor, and would not give up trying. Delightfully, he brought with him the chime clock, piano and other rare treasure that he had specially gotten ready to present to the emperor. Traveling with him on his third trip to Beijing was a Spanish Jesuit named Diego de Pantoja, who was recommended by Alessandro Valignano.

What he did not expect was a repetition of the same problem he encountered in his previous attempts to visit

弘海的帮助下，他在南京买了一所房子，作好了长期等待的打算。平日里，他继续与南京的知识阶层广泛交往，扩大自己的影响，并尽可能地向他们传播天主教教义和西方知识。

南京是明王朝的故都。虽然1422年已经迁都北京，可南京仍然保留着一整套与北京同样的行政体系，以及曾经作为首都的宏伟外观。熟悉了南京，将会大大方便将来进入北京后的传教事业。因此，利玛窦对南京进行了细致入微的观察。南京城里那些高大的建筑，数不清的庙宇、宝塔和桥梁，才华横溢的士人，举止文雅的市民，甚至于土地肥沃、风景秀丽的南京郊区，都让利玛窦赞不绝口。他把南京誉为"不仅在中国，哪怕在整个东方，都是第一位的城市"。南京的内阁、六部等行政机构，他也尽可能地去深入了解，为今后在北京拓展局面作准备。虽然还不知道什么时候能再次进京，但利玛窦满怀宗教的热诚，坚定不移地相信，一定会有那么一天，他会在北京接受中国皇帝的召见，并且通过对皇帝的影响，让中国人都成为耶稣的子民。

利玛窦并没有等待太久。一年后，北上的机遇

Missionary in Confucian Garb

南京明城墙遗址。在说及南京城之大时，利玛窦引用了当地人讲的一个故事：两个人从城的相反方向骑马相对而行，花了一整天时间才相遇。
The historic site of Nanjing's Ming city walls. When discussing the size of Nanjing, Matteo Ricci quoted a local story: two people riding towards each other from the opposite directions of the city would take one whole day to meet.

Beijing. Japan continued its advances into Korea, and the Ming government discontinued all trade activities with foreigner nations, and sent soldiers on surveillance and to search for Japanese spies all across the city. As Matteo Ricci was a foreigner, he almost got himself arrested, if not for the help of his friends.

Over the past 19 years, all the Chinese friends that Matteo Ricci made had always come to his rescue at the most crucial moments. When on his way to Jining, Shandong, Matteo Ricci met a good friend, Li Zhi, whom

又向他招手了。他的朋友祝世禄帮他办好了所有手续,并安排他乘坐押运丝绸贡品的船只进京。利玛窦已经在中国不屈不挠地准备了19年,这次,他下定决心,不见到皇帝本人,决不罢休!他兴高采烈地携带着为中国皇帝精心准备的自鸣钟、西洋琴等珍贵礼物,与范礼安推荐的西班牙传教士庞迪我(Diego de Pantoja)一道,第三次踏上了前往北京的征途。

不料,这次又赶上他眼中"好战的日本"入侵朝鲜。明朝不仅因此中断了与外国的贸易,还派出官兵到处监视、抓捕日本特务。因为是外国人,利玛窦差点儿被抓进监狱,幸亏朋友相助,才得以脱身。

在过去的19年里利玛窦结识的那些中国朋友,总会在关键时刻帮上他的忙。途径山东济宁时,利玛窦遇上了在南京认识的好友李贽。李贽当时正住在漕运总督刘东星家。刘东星见利玛窦准备呈给皇帝的奏折写得不太合规矩,便亲自帮利玛窦重新起草奏折,又写了好几封推荐信,为利玛窦引荐自己在北京的朋友。由于刘东星的地位与名望,这些信函在后来给了利玛窦很大的帮助。

一路十分顺利,直到船行至山东临清。负责在临

he had gotten to know in Nanjing. At that time, Li Zhi was staying at the residence of the Governor-General of Water Transportation, Liu Dongxing. Liu Dongxing happened to read the memorial Matteo Ricci had written to the emperor. He felt that it was not appropriately composed, and personally helped him to rewrite another. He also wrote a few letters of recommendation to his friends in Beijing. As Liu Dongxing was a man of considerable reputation and status, these letters became very helpful to Matteo Ricci.

The voyage went on smoothly, until the boat arrived at Linqing, Shandong. Ma Tang, a eunuch who was in charge of tax collection in Linqing, was a corrupt and greedy official. He was aware that Matteo Ricci had with him many rare and expensive treasures for the emperor, and tried to exploit him. First, he deliberately delayed Matteo Ricci and company, bringing them to Tianjin. The officials at the imperial palace soon received the news that a foreign priest was waiting with tributes in Tianjin and sent for an inventory of the tributes. However, upon submitting the inventory list, there was no reply from the palace for several weeks. Ma Tang lost his patience and became increasingly unfriendly with Matteo Ricci and his company. He locked them in a temple and placed them under guard.

As Ma Tang did not gain anything from Matteo Ricci, he accused him of not submitting a full inventory of his tributes to the emperor. He ordered for their luggage to be

清监管税收的马堂，是一个贪婪的太监。马堂见利玛窦他们准备进贡给皇帝的礼物都十分珍贵，便企图从这些外国传教士身上为自己捞些好处。他将利玛窦一行人带到天津。宫里得知有外国传教士带着礼品在天津等候，下旨让呈上一份礼品清单。可清单送上去后等了几个星期，始终没有回音。马堂对利玛窦等人的态度变得越来越不客气，下令将他们关到一所庙里，派士兵日夜看守。

马堂没能得到足够的好处，就故意挑毛病说利玛窦他们还有隐瞒未报的礼品，下令将他们所有的行李都打开来接受检查。当马堂发现其中的基督受难像时，他惊诧而愤怒地喊道："这是什么？你们是想用

秦淮河风光。千百年来，秦淮河一直是南京最繁华的地方之一。利玛窦在其回忆录中对它也作过介绍。
Scenery of Qinhuai River. For thousands of years, Qinhuai River had been the most prosperous place in Nanjing. Matteo Ricci had mentioned it in his memoir.

checked. When Ma Tang saw the portrait of the Passion of Christ, he was shocked and enraged, accusing Matteo Ricci of cursing the Ming emperor.

In his broken Mandarin, Diego de Pantoja explained to Ma Tang who Jesus Christ was, and how He is who came to earth to save mankind of their sins, and how He was resurrected and rose to Heaven.

Of course, Ma Tang was unable to understand what Diego de Pantoja said, and it provoked him further. He decided to report these foreigners' misdeeds to the emperor, and swore to put them behind bars.

Matteo Ricci understood that for the Chinese people who did not believe in Jesus Christ, it would be pointless attempting to explain to them. His friends had also warned him that Ma Tang was not one to be meddled with, as the emperor would always go to the eunuchs to get things done. Matteo Ricci now found himself caught in a precarious situation, and sank into despair.

Even when failure looms, there is always hope. As Matteo Ricci was at his wits' end, there was a turn for the better—the Ming emperor had summoned him to Beijing with his tributes.

On 24 January 1601, Matteo Ricci finally came to Beijing. Even though he was unclear about the future, he was confident that he would gain the approval of the emperor to preach in China.

它来诅咒我们伟大的皇帝吗？"

庞迪我用不熟练的汉语向他解释说："这是我们的上帝。他创造了世间万物，给了我们生命，又为了救赎人类的罪孽而死去。他死之后，凭借自己的力量复活，升入了天堂。"

马堂无法理解庞迪我的话。他更加暴跳如雷地表示，要把这些外国人的罪恶报告给皇帝，将他们打入天牢！

利玛窦知道，对于不相信耶稣的中国人，再怎么解释也没有用。而且他的朋友早就劝告过他，像马堂这样的太监不能轻易得罪，因为皇帝做任何事情都要通过这些太监。此时的利玛窦进退维艰，陷入深深的绝望中。

中国有句古诗，"山穷水尽疑无路，柳暗花明又一村"。正当利玛窦一筹莫展之时，事情突然有了转机——万历皇帝颁下圣旨，召利玛窦等人携所带贡物马上进京！

1601年1月24日，利玛窦终于正式进入北京！虽然前途还是未知，但他满怀信心，一定能获得皇帝的恩准，在中国传播天主教。

Early Development of Catholicism in China

As early as the Tang Dynasty (618–907), missionaries of the Nestorian order, a Catholic denomination, were once dispatched to China from Persia, and were warmly received by the Emperor Taizong (reigned 627–649) of the Tang Dynasty.

The emperor even sent the prime minister outside the city to welcome the Nestorian missionary Alopen Abraham, who was placed in a special accommodation to translate Catholic classics. The Nestorians were very popular in the early Tang Dynasty and was highly regarded by the imperial court. The Christians interacted with the high and mighty, securing a prominent position. Later, as Emperor Wuzong (reigned 841–846) was eradicating Buddhism in the country, the Nestorians were mistaken as a branch of Buddhism and suffered a heavy blow.

During the Yuan Dynasty (1206–1368), the Nestorian enjoyed a brief revival in China. At this time, Odorico da Pordenone, Giovannida Montecorvino and other Catholic missionaries also came to China. But as the Yuan Dynasty was overthrown by the Ming Dynasty, the Catholic mission in China was dissolved once again.

早期天主教在中国的发展

早在唐代（618—907），天主教的一支——聂斯托里派就曾经从波斯来到中国，并且受到唐太宗（627—649在位）的热情接待。唐太宗派遣宰相亲自去城外迎接聂斯托里派的传道人阿罗本（Alopen Abraham），并将他安置到专门的住处让，他翻译带来的天主教经典。聂斯托里派在唐初很受朝廷重视，教徒和高官显贵交往，地位显赫。后来，因唐武宗（841—846在位）铲除佛教，聂斯托里派被误认为是佛教分支，一并遭到沉重打击。

元代（1206—1368），聂斯托里派在中国一度短暂复兴。此时，鄂多立克（Odorico da Pordenone）、孟德高维诺（Giovannida Montecorvino）等天主教传教士也来到中国。但随着元朝被明朝推翻，天主教在中国取得的传教成果很快又化为烟尘。

IV

Taking Root in Beijing

Matteo Ricci's passage into Beijing was not a smooth course. Caught in the political center of China, it was unavoidable that he and the other Jesuit priests got involved in the political tussles.

First, they stayed at the residence of Ma Tang, located outside the south of the city. Originally, based on what was written, any matter involving foreigners should be taken care of by the Board of Rites, but Ma Tang and a group of other eunuchs all wanted to make some gains out of it and hence, they overrode the authority of the Board of Rites. They reported directly to the emperor, hoping to be commended by the emperor for their initiatives, and to receive part of the reward that the emperor would be bestowing Matteo Ricci. The officials from the Board of Rites were very unhappy about it, and the two parties clashed. In the end, the Board of Rites took Matteo Ricci and the Jesuits out of Ma Tang's house and arranged for them to stay with the other foreign envoys visiting Beijing.

4

皇帝上宾，扎根京城

奉旨进京之后，利玛窦等人的处境并不顺利。身处中国的政治中心，他们不可避免地被卷入了朝臣的争斗之中。

他们先被安排住在南城外马堂家里。本来按照规定，涉及外国人的事宜应由礼部管理。但马堂等太监却想在这件事上插上一脚，绕过礼部，直接向皇帝汇报，以博取皇帝的夸奖，并借机贪污皇帝赐给进贡者的赏金。礼部官员对此自然十分不满，两派势力的冲突达到白热化。最终礼部派出一队官兵，将利玛窦等人从马堂家里带走，安排他们和来北京的外国使节住在一起。

几天后，利玛窦终于得到通知，进宫觐见皇帝。他们与前来朝贡的外国使者一道，由身着华丽朝服的中国官员陪同，在上千人的仪仗队护送下，浩浩荡荡

Missionary in Confucian Garb

A few days later, Matteo Ricci was summoned into the imperial palace for an audience with the emperor. He and the other Jesuits, as well as other foreign envoys, were escorted by a retinue elegantly dressed officials and up to a thousand guards of honor into the Forbidden City. However, they were overwhelmingly disappointed to find out that they did not get to meet the emperor at all. Once in the palace, they were asked to bow to the emperor's throne, and present their gifts. This was because since 1585, the Ming Emperor Wanli had announced that he would not be appearing in court. He would not meet with anyone else, other than his family and the eunuchs.

利玛窦献给万历皇帝的礼物：《圣母子像》
Matteo Ricci's present to Emperor Wanli: "Virgin Mary and Infant Jesus."

Of the multitude of tributes presented to the emperor, the most special ones were the European items presented by Matteo Ricci. As not many Europeans were allowed into China back then, such European items were

地进入紫禁城。不过，他们压根就没见到皇帝的真容，只是对着皇帝的宝座行礼、进献礼物。因为从1585年起，万历皇帝就宣布不再上朝，甚至不见家人和太监以外的任何人。

在来自各国的众多礼物中，利玛窦他们献上的西洋物品显得非常特别。因为当时很少有欧洲人能够进入中国，即便是中国皇帝，见到这些来自遥远的欧罗巴的礼物也觉得稀罕珍贵。

利玛窦进献的礼品包括：油画三幅（包括天主像一幅、圣母像两幅）、天主经一本、世界地图一张、西洋琴一架、玻璃棱镜两个、镶宝石的十字架一个以及西洋银币若干，还有一大一小两座铜制自鸣钟。

最令万历皇帝着迷的，还是自鸣钟。他下令在宫中专门为大自鸣钟修建一座雄伟的钟楼，而对那座精巧的小钟更是看了又看，爱不释手。皇太后听说有洋人进献了这么个奇物后，派人来借去赏玩。万历皇帝担心会有借无还，暗中命令太监偷偷把发条弄松。果然，皇太后发现这个西洋玩意儿走着走着指针就停下不动后，便对它失去了兴趣。暗自高兴的皇帝马上派人将它拿回来，上好发条，重新放回自己的寝宫。作

considered rare treasures even for the Chinese emperor.

Among the tributes presented by Matteo Ricci were three oil paintings of Jesus and Mother Mary, one Holy Bible, one world map, one piano, two glass prisms, a bejeweled crucifix, a number of European coins, and two chime clocks—one large and one small—both made of copper.

What actually captured the heart of Emperor Wanli were the chime clocks. He ordered for a clock tower to be built in the palace to house the bigger clock, and was inseparable from the small one, which was exquisite in design. When the Empress Dowager heard of such an interesting item, she sent for it. Emperor Wanli was worried that his mother would not return it to him, so he secretly instructed his eunuch to loosen the spiral spring in the clock. Just as he expected, when the Empress Dowager saw that the pointers in the clock stopped after a while, she lost interest in it. The emperor was delighted that his plan worked and ordered for it to return to him. He tightened the spiral spring, and placed the clock in his bedroom. As compensation, he gave the painting of Virgin Mary to the Empress Dowager, who was a devout Buddhist.

The chime clocks needed regular maintenance, but none of the people in the palace knew how to do it. Each time when the clocks needed repair or maintenance, the

为补偿，他将利玛窦进献的圣母像送给了笃信佛教的皇太后。

自鸣钟需要定期维修，而宫中无人会这项技术，每次只能由太监将钟抬到宫外利玛窦居住的四夷馆去，十分不方便。于是皇帝下令：自鸣钟今后不许拿出宫，有需要时，召西洋人进宫修理。利玛窦因此得到可以经常进出皇宫的特权，可他始终没能见到皇帝本人。

万历皇帝像
Portrait of Emperor Wanli.

万历皇帝其实也很想亲眼看看这个传说中长相很特别的外国人，但他既然已经表示过连自己的大臣都不见，自然也不能破例见外国人了。想来想去，万历皇帝有了主意。他派去两个画家，给利玛窦画了张像，再拿回给他看。这样就既不违背誓言，又满足了他的好奇心。不过这样一来，利玛窦此前的梦想彻底破灭了——要想打动中国皇帝，获得他对天主教的支

eunuchs would carry them to Matteo Ricci's residence to have them fixed. It was very inconvenient. Hence, the emperor ordered that the clocks were not to be taken out of the palace; the foreigner would be summoned into the palace to fix the clocks instead. Because of this, Matteo Ricci received the special privilege to go into the palace regularly. Yet, he still did not get the chance to meet with the emperor. In fact, the emperor was very keen to meet with this foreigner, whom he had heard looked rather interesting. He felt that since he was not even seeing his own officials, it was not appropriate to make such an exception. After much consideration, he came out with an idea, and sent two painters to Matteo Ricci and had his portrait done. In this way, he was able to find out how the foreigner looked like, without having to go back on his words. This, however, was a blow to Matteo Ricci. It completely dashed his hopes of ever meeting the emperor, and seeking his support to preach in China. It would be impossible to even convert the emperor.

The piano presented by Matteo Ricci was also popular with the emperor for a period of time. Emperor Wanli had chosen a few young and intelligent eunuchs, and sent them to Matteo Ricci to learn to play the piano for a month. Matteo Ricci also composed a few easy tunes and with the help of a Chinese poet who had converted to Catholicism, they wrote a hymm and taught the eunuchs

穿儒服的传教士

利玛窦献给万历皇帝的礼物：他绘制的《堪舆万国全图》。该图于明万历三十年（1602）在北京付印，在当时社会产生了很大影响。
Matteo Ricci's present to Emperor Wanli: the world map illustrated by him in China. It was reprinted in Beijing in 1602 during the Ming Dynasty. It had a significant impact on China's society at that time.

持，甚至发展他本人入教，已经根本没有可能。

　　利玛窦献上的西洋琴也在宫中流行一时。万历皇帝挑选出几个年轻、聪明的小太监，让他们跟着利玛窦和庞迪我学习了一个月西洋音乐。利玛窦还亲自谱写了几支简单的曲子，让一位皈依天主教的中国诗人填上歌词，取名《天乐正音》，教太监用他进献的西方乐器弹奏、演唱。直到今天，北京的天主教堂还在继续演唱这些歌曲。

　　那幅世界地图则被下令悬挂在皇帝的寝宫。每天

Missionary in Confucian Garb

how to play it with the musical instruments he presented to the emperor. The songs that Matteo Ricci composed are still being played today in the Catholic churches in Beijing.

The world map was hung in the emperor's bedroom, and every night before he went to bed, Emperor Wanli would spend sometime looking at it and ponder on it a while.

In the memorial that Matteo Ricci had written to Emperor Wanli, he expressed that he had traveled a long distance to China, and being interested in China and its cultures, he willingly put himself through perilous journey to China that took him three years. He had also waited patiently in Guangdong for 15 long years, learning the Chinese language and culture. In Nanchang and Nanjing, he spent five years learning to write in Chinese, and introduced the Chinese classical writings to the West. All he hoped to achieve in Beijing was to be at the service of the emperor with his knowledge in astronomy, geography and mathematics.

Such heartfelt honesty greatly impressed Emperor Wanli and his trust in this foreign priest, Hence, despite the several requests from conservative officials to evict Matteo Ricci from Beijing, Emperor Wanli had not approved a single one. On the contrary, he allowed Matteo Ricci to reside in Beijing permanently, and bestowed him

晚上，万历都要在地图前仔细察看，怀想一番才去睡觉。

在利玛窦呈给万历皇帝的奏折中，他表明自己不远万里前来中国，是受到中华文明的感召，因此不惜花费三年时间，经过艰险的旅程到达中国，又耐心地在广东居住了15年，学习中文和中国文化，还在南昌和南京用了五年学习中文写作，并将中国典籍介绍到西方。他只希望能留在京城，用自己精通的天文、地理和数学知识为皇帝服务。

这些忠诚的表白博得了皇帝的欢心和信任。因此，尽管朝廷里一些保守的官员几次上书，要求赶走利玛窦，万历皇帝都没有批准。相反，他不但恩准利玛窦长住北京，还赐地让利玛窦修建教堂。

古老的中国终于微微地向利玛窦打开了大门。皇帝允许他们在京城里居住建堂，也就在某种程度上意味着他们可以在中国传教。那些分布在各地的传教士也因此可以更加放心地吸收中国民众入教，而不必随时担心地方官员的责难与干涉。

随后的十年，利玛窦安居北京。不过，他始终只是被皇帝当作一名御用钟表匠和宫廷乐师，为此他每

Missionary in Confucian Garb

a plot of land on which he could build his church.

With the blessings of Emperor Wanli, China finally opened its door into its ancient world. By giving the approval to the Jesuits to build their church and reside in Beijing, to a certain extent, it also meant that they were allowed to preach in China. The Jesuits who were spread across China could then preach freely to the people and convert them to Catholicism, without worrying about the interference and censure created by the local officials.

For the next 10 years, Matteo Ricci led a peaceful life in Beijing. Despite that, he continued to be regarded as a clockmaker and a musician of the imperial palace. For his service, he was entitled to 12 pieces of silver every month. He was still unable to achieve his objective of converting the emperor of China, in order to convert the entire Chinese Empire as a Catholic nation.

Matteo Ricci had hoped to achieve his mission objective through converting the high society of China. It was a renaissance period for the Chinese society at that time, and many intellectual and educated people who were greatly interested in Matteo Ricci and the heterogeneous ideas that he brought with him. At the same time, the special treatment that Matteo Ricci received from the emperor also alleviated his reputation and standing in the Chinese society, and many nobilities were proud to befriend him. Many visitors thronged Matteo Ricci's

穿儒服的传教士

西方人笔下的中国风情画：17世纪的北京
Western artists' impression of Beijing in the 17th century.

月可以领取12两银子的皇家俸禄。他无从实施耶稣会的计划——通过最高统治者的归化，让整个中华大帝国成为上帝的国度。

利玛窦转而希望通过感化中国的上流社会来达到传教目的。当时的中国社会正好处在一个思想革新时期，很多知识分子对于利玛窦和他带来的异质思想抱有兴趣。同时，皇帝给予的特殊待遇也在无形中增加了利玛窦的声望，很多达官显贵都以能与他交往为

Missionary in Confucian Garb

residence. Some of the visitors were Matteo Ricci's long-time friends, others were new friends who had admired his reputation. The local officials and scholars who were in the capital for the imperial examination were all interested to meet with him. Matteo Ricci had never declined anyone's request to meet with him. Every day, his schedule would be packed to the max, frequently receiving up to 20 or more guests. He was so busy that he missed

北京南堂铜版画
Copper engraving of Beijing's South Church.

his meals. If it happened to be a festival, such as the Lunar New Year, he would be out visiting his friends. In a single day, he would chat with more than a hundred people, which was a record for him. All this visitations drained a significant portion of Matteo Ricci's time and energy. However, all these meetings were necessary. Matteo Ricci had the understanding that many visitors to Beijing were the elites of China. If he could preach a little each time he talked to them, eventually, he believed, they would be

穿儒服的传教士

荣。利玛窦的住所前,前来拜访他的车辆络绎不绝,其中既有他以前的旧相识,也有慕名而来的新朋友。来京城朝觐皇帝的地方官员和参加科举考试的读书人,都想见见利玛窦。对于这些请求,利玛窦从来都不会拒绝。他的日程总是安排得满满当当,常常一天要接见20多个客人,忙得连饭都顾不上吃。遇到新年

今天人们见到的南堂,是在利玛窦修建的教堂基础上改修、扩建而成。
Present-day South Church. Alterations and extensions were made on the foundation of the church built by Matteo Ricci.

led to convert to Catholicism. And for all the people who had encountered the sincerity, friendliness, wisdom and farsightedness, they would spread his good reputation in their respective hometowns. Indeed, at that time, every person in every province in China had heard of Matteo Ricci, and people would discuss about his knowledge and religion.

In 1605, under the leadership of Matteo Ricci, the church located inside Xuanwu Gate of Beijing was constructed. It is the first Catholic church that was built in Beijing. Subsequently, it went through several rounds of renovation and expansion, and remains the main church of Beijing's Catholic diocese. In Beijing, it was fondly referred to as "Nan Tang" or "South Church."

或其它重要节日，他还得出门拜访，最多时一天要与上百人寒暄或谈话。每天的迎来送往，耗费了利玛窦大量的时间和精力。可是，这些会见又是必不可少的。利玛窦深知，来到京城的人很多都是中国社会的精英，在与他们的谈话中传播天主教思想，通过一点一滴的接触、渗透，便有可能引领他们接受天主教。而这些人在亲身领会了利玛窦的真诚、友好和睿智后，回到各自家乡，将利玛窦的美名进一步传扬。于是乎，在当时中国的每一个省，都有人在谈论利玛窦和他的知识、他的宗教。

在利玛窦主持下，1605年，坐落于宣武门内的教堂建成，这是北京历史上的第一座天主堂。教堂后来几经改修、扩建，至今仍是天主教北京教区的主教座堂，也就是人们常说的"南堂"。

忙里抽闲，利玛窦还将自己在中国多年的传教经历整理出来，撰写成回忆录。

Francois Xavier—the First Jesuit to Arrive in China

Francois Xavier was born in Spain in 1506. His father was the king's personal adviser, and his mother was from a noble family. In 1540, Xavier became one of the first Jesuit missionaries, and was dispatched to preach in East India, Japan and other places countries. He preached in Japan for more than two years, and learned that Japanese culture was greatly influenced by China. It was this realization that initiated his idea of preaching in China.

At that time, other than foreign envoys on diplomatic mission, the Ming government banned all foreigners from entering China. Francois Xavier made several attempts, and finally arrived in Shangchuan Island off the coast of Taishan, Guangdong, and became the first Jesuit to arrive in China. However, he was not able to gain entry to the Chinese mainland, and died in December 1552 on Shangchuan Island. He was later buried in India in 1662, and was officially regarded as a saint by the Church.

Francois Xavier raised the idea of converting the Chinese empire to Christianity, which became the main objective of generations of Western missionaries. Perhaps it was a historical coincidence, but two months after the death of Francois Xavier, Matteo Ricci was born. Many years later, Matteo Ricci completed Francois Xavier's unfinished missionary work in China.

最早进入中国的耶稣会士沙勿略

方济各·沙勿略（Francois Xavier），1506年出生于西班牙。他的父亲是国王的私人顾问，母亲也出身名门。1540年，沙勿略成为耶稣会的首批传教士，奉命前往东方的印度、日本等地传教。沙勿略在日本传教两年多，得知日本文化深受中国影响，因此萌生了到中国传播福音的想法。

当时，除了官方正式派遣的使节外，明朝政府禁止一切外国人进入中国。沙勿略想方设法，终于在1551年到达广东台山沿海的上川岛，成为最早进入中国的耶稣会士。但沙勿略一直未能进入中国内地。1552年12月，他病逝在上川岛，后来被安葬在印度，1662年被教会列为圣徒。

沙勿略提出的使整个中华帝国天主教化的设想，成为西方一代又一代传教士为之奋斗的重要目标。或许是历史的巧合，就在沙勿略病逝后2个月，利玛窦诞生了。若干年后，利玛窦完成了沙勿略在中国未尽的传教事业。

V

Connecting the East and West through Friendship

Matteo Ricci resided in China for 28 years, and traveled widely within the country. As such, he made so many friends that those that could be recorded by their names numbered more than a hundred.

Not long after Matteo Ricci arrived in Zhaoqing, he befriended Qu Taisu, who not only was a friend, but was also Matteo Ricci's student. Matteo Ricci taught Qu Taisu his knowledge in the elements, and hoped that he would translate all the mathematical knowledge of the West into Chinese, in order that it would reach out to more Chinese people. But Qu Taisu, who was varied in his areas of interests, had only managed to translate the first volume of Euclid's *Elements* into Chinese, before he went to live his drifter's life, traveling from place to place. However, Qu Taisu did make use of his connection in his wide social circle to spread the name of Matteo Ricci wherever he traveled to.

5

广交朋友，汇通中西

利玛窦在中国生活了28年，辗转各地，结交了数不清的朋友。其中，有可靠文字记载的就有100多人。

利玛窦到肇庆后不久，就认识了瞿太素。后来，瞿太素不仅成为了利玛窦的朋友，还成为了他的弟子。利玛窦传授给瞿太素几何知识，希望他能够将这些西方数学知识翻译成中文，传播给更多的中国人。但兴趣广泛的瞿太素只将欧几里得《几何原本》第一卷部分译成中文后，就继续他的云游生活去了。不过，瞿太素凭借自己的社会关系，为利玛窦在全国积累了广泛的人脉，而且他每云游到一个地方，就会在当地宣传利玛窦的学问和人品。

在肇庆，利玛窦还见过中国著名的戏剧家汤显祖。汤显祖为此专门作了两首诗，诗中对利玛窦的长相和他的宗教都细加描绘，成为一段文坛佳话。

In Zhaoqing, Matteo Ricci met the famous Chinese playwright Tang Xianzu, who composed two poems specially for Matteo Ricci. The poems, which described in detail the looks of Matteo Ricci and his religion, became one of the best ever written of him.

It would not be wrong to say that almost all the greatest figures in China's literary circle had directly or indirectly been connected with Matteo Ricci. This was a fact that was more apparent when Matteo Ricci went to Nanchang, Nanjing and Beijing.

In Nanchang, Matteo Ricci referred to himself as the "Western Confucian," meaning, the Confucian scholar from the West. He befriended Prince Jian An and Prince Le An, relatives of the imperial family. Matteo Ricci became a regular guest at the two princes' residences. To show his appreciation for them both, he wrote and dedicated to them the book, *on Friendship,* sharing with them his ideas on friendship. In his book, he quoted about 100 famous lines on friendship from the West based solely on his amazing memory. What Matteo Ricci did not expect was the book became a best seller when it was published, and was popular among the nobles and the poor scholars alike. He wrote to his friends in Europe and told them how this book had helped to enhance his reputation as a gifted scholar, and a wise and moral character.

Once, at a banquet, Matteo Ricci read and memorized a

可以说，同时代中国最伟大的文化名人，几乎都与利玛窦有过直接或者间接的交往。这点在利玛窦进入南昌、南京和北京后，表现得更加明显。

在南昌，利玛窦自称"西儒"，也就是从西方来的儒士。他结识了明朝皇室建安王朱多㸅和乐安王朱多㷆。两位王爷经常邀请利玛窦到王府做客。为了表示对他们的谢意，利玛窦写了一部谈论友情的著作《交友论》。凭借惊人的记忆力，他在书中引用了100句关于友谊的西方名言。出乎利玛窦意料的是，书一出版，竟然受到了中国士人的广泛欢迎，上自达官显贵，下到寒门学子，都对来自西方的友谊格言深感兴趣，并且广为传颂。利玛窦在写给欧洲朋友的信中说："我在机械制造方面的才能已经受到了人们的赞

利玛窦《交友论》书影
Matteo Ricci's *On Friendship*.

list of 400 Chinese characters, reciting the list accordingly, from top to bottom, and the other way round. The guests were all stunned by his amazing memory. At the request of the inspector-general of Jiangxi, Lu Wangai, Matteo Ricci published the book, *Treatise on Mnemonic Arts*, and shared with the Chinese people Western techniques of memory. This completely changed the perception that the educated people had of him—Matteo Ricci was not only a Western monk, who brought with him all sorts of interesting and strange looking Western gadgets, but he was also a knowledgeable and educated person. An increasing number of people who admired and respected him began to stream to him and requested to be his students.

During the spring of 1600, Matteo Ricci befriended Xu Guangqi in Nanjing. Xu Guangqi would become one of the the most significant friend that he would ever have in China.

Actually, when Matteo Ricci was still staying in Zhaoqing, Xu Guangqi had visited him once, but Matteo Ricci was not home at that time. Four years after that day, two men finally met, and hit it off immediately. At that time, Xu Guangqi was only an ordinary student, but he was knowledgeable, and had the deep realization that for the Ming Dynasty to become powerful, it must acquire more knowledge about the world and rule

扬,而这篇文章给我带来了有天分的学者、有道德的贤人的声誉。这篇文章非常受欢迎,已经在两个地方出版了。"

一次宴会中,利玛窦在将400个毫不相关的汉字浏览了一遍之后,居然将它们全部按照顺序背了下来,然后又将它们按照相反顺序倒背如流!在场的所有人都惊呆了。

应江西巡抚陆万垓的要求,利玛窦把他的惊人记忆术总结成文字,写成《西国记法》一书,教那些想在科举考试中取得好成绩的考生怎样提高记忆力。这更让中国的知识分子对他刮目相看。原来利玛窦不光是万里之外来的"洋和尚",也不只带来了些稀奇古怪的洋玩意儿,他还有这么渊博的知识、这么精深的学问!尊敬、欣赏他,想跟他交朋友,或者拜他为师的人越来越多。

1600年的春天,利玛窦在南京认识了徐光启。后来,徐光启成为他在中国最重要的朋友之一。其实当利玛窦还在肇庆时,徐光启就曾经慕名前去造访,可惜利玛窦恰好不在。时隔四年,两人首次见面,就一见如故,相谈甚欢。当时的徐光启还只是一名普通读

the country with it. He was greatly amazed by Matteo Ricci's knowledge in natural science, and approached him to teach him more on about astronomy, the calendar system, mathematics, and measurement, etc. Under the influence of Matteo Ricci, Xu Guangqi converted to Catholicism, and was baptized in Nanjing in 1603. The following year, Xu Guangqi successfully passed his imperial examination, and was appointed as a court official in Beijing. He was later promoted and became a scholar of Wenyuan Chamber. In Beijing, Matteo Ricci and Xu Guangqi spent time more time together, studying Western knowledge. Xu Guangqi also assisted Matteo Ricci in the translation of several Western literary works to the Chinese language. Among these works was Euclid's *Elements*, which Qu Taisu left unfinished. The book was completed and published in 1607, and had a profound impact on the development of mathematics in China. Many mathematical terms that were used in the book are still in use today.

In Nanjing, Matteo Ricci also got to know another important friend, Li Zhi, who was a great thinker of the later Ming Dynasty. He advocated the abolishment of the feudal traditions, and questioned Confucius' teachings, and called for individual liberation and freedom. These radical views were not welcomed by the authority, and Li Zhi was put into prison when he was well over 70

书人，但他极具见识，深刻认识到明王朝要想强盛，必须发展"经世治用"的实用之学。他对利玛窦丰富的自然科学知识大为叹服，主动向利玛窦学习天文、历法、数学、测量等学问。在利玛窦的影响下，1603年，徐光启在南京接受洗礼，成为天主教徒。1604年，徐光启考中进士，入京做官，最后官至文渊阁大学士。在北京，两人过往更加密切，常常在一起研究西学。徐光启还协助利玛窦将一些西方著作翻译成中文，其中最重要的就是欧几里得的《几何原本》。利玛窦和徐光启一起翻译了该书的前六卷，于1607年付梓，对中国数学的发展产生了重要影响。书中的许多名词，如点、线、面、三角形、平行线、直角、锐角、钝角等，一直沿用至今。

在南京，利玛窦还结识了另一位重要朋友——李贽。李贽是明代后期的一位大思

李贽（1527—1602），明代著名思想家。
Li Zhi (1527-1602), the famous thinker of the Ming Dynasty.

Missionary in Confucian Garb

years of age. In the end, he committed suicide in prison, instead of compromising with the authority and expression his displeasure of the autocratic political system. Undoubtedly, for such a radical and open-minded revolutionary like Li Zhi, Matteo Ricci and his Western ideas were great attractions. Li Zhi, who was a leading scholar in the education realm, had paid personal visits to Matteo Ricci, and he described the Jesuit priest as a fine-looking man. He not only wrote poems praising Matteo Ricci's intelligence, scholarly manner and knowledge, but he also commissioned and made copies of *on Friendship*, and distributed them to his students all across the nation. However, Li Zhi was puzzled by Matteo Ricci's celibacy. He did not understand why he would travel such a long journey to China, not wanting to get married and have a family, yet wanting to remain in this Oriental country.

徐光启 (1562—1633)，明代杰出的科学家，中国引进西方近代科学技术的先驱之一。
Xu Guangqi (1562-1633), outstanding scientist of the Ming Dynasty, one of the pioneers who imported the Western modern science and technology to China.

想家，他主张反对封建传统，质疑孔子的儒家正统观念，提倡个性解放和自由。李贽的特立独行不为当权者所容，在他70多岁高龄时还被抓进监狱。最后，他在狱中用剃刀自刭，以决绝的不妥协态度表达对专制政治的不满。像这样具有开放、先进思想的中国人，自然会被利玛窦和他的西方思想吸引。李贽以学界泰斗的身份，亲自上门拜访利玛窦，并称赞利玛窦是"第一标致人"。他不仅写诗赞美利玛窦的聪明、儒雅和博学，还请人抄写了许多份《交友论》，分赠给自己在各地的众多弟子。李贽对利玛窦的赞美很快在社会上传开，间接促进了天主教在全中国的传播。不过，李贽始终弄不明白，是什么让利玛窦不远万里来到中国，也不结婚生子，一心一意待在这个东方国度？要知道，那时

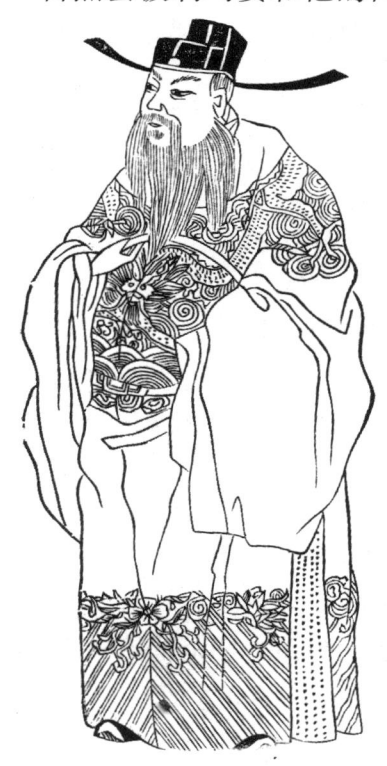

李之藻（1565—1630），明代科学家，17世纪中西文化交流史上的重要人物。
Li Zhizao (1565-1630), scientist of the Ming Dynasty, an important 17th-century figure in the history of East-West cultural exchange.

Missionary in Confucian Garb

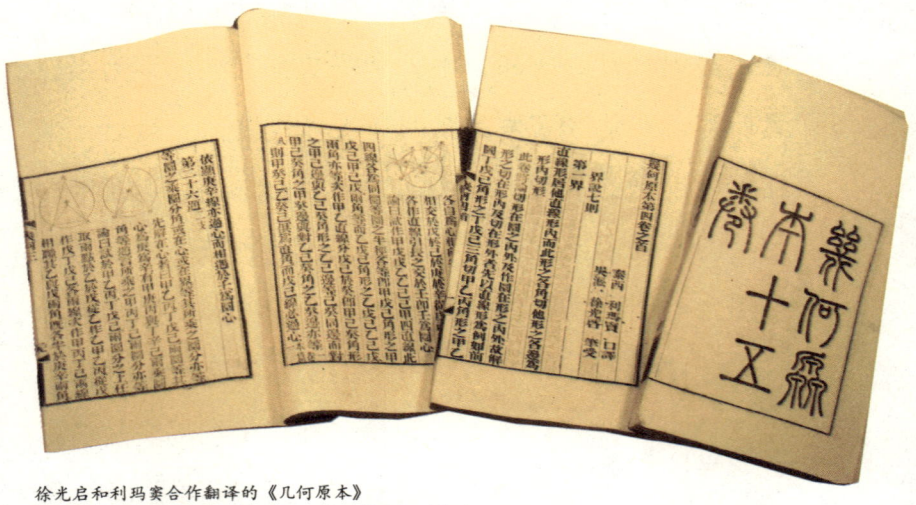

徐光启和利玛窦合作翻译的《几何原本》
Elements co-translated by Xu Guangqi and Matteo Ricci.

What he did not know, of course, was that Matteo Ricci was in China to preach and change the beliefs of the people in Confucianism, and convert to Catholicism instead. This was a secret that was staunchly guarded by Matteo Ricci.

During his stay in Nanjing, Matteo Ricci socialized regularly with many high-ranking officials and distinguished individuals. He even had a debate with several high monks, and won the debate with its radical argument grounded in science. His residence in the west of Nanjing became a popular gathering place for many learned men. There, Matteo Ricci discussed astronomy, calendar systems, geography, and other scientific

欧几里得《几何原本》原书书影
The original *Elements*, authored by Euclid.

利玛窦还不敢告诉任何人，他来中国是为了传播基督的精神，想让中华帝国改变几千年来对儒家文化的信仰，转向对上帝的崇拜。

在南京居住期间，利玛窦与当地许多高官名士都有往来。利玛窦还与著名高僧、大报恩寺的三淮和尚进行了一场辩论，并凭借科学的思辨赢得了胜利。他在南京城西的住所成为当地士大夫聚谈的重要场地。

Missionary in Confucian Garb

利玛窦与徐光启
Matteo Ricci and Xu Guangqi.

knowledge with them. These topics had for generations, eluded the educated Chinese.

In his written report to the Jesuits in Europe, Matteo Ricci summarized the reasons of his popularity as the following. First, it was because the locals had not encountered any Western man before him, hence, they were curious about him. Second, he had an amazing memory, which many Chinese wanted to learn from him. Thirdly, it was because of his abilities to make use of the Chinese classical teachings to preach the Catholic

在那里，利玛窦与他们一起讨论天文、历算、地理等自然科学知识，而这些都是历来被中国知识分子普遍忽视的知识。

在写给耶稣会总部的报告中，利玛窦这样总结自己出名的主要原因：一是因为很多中国人从没有见过外国人；二是他的记忆力非常好，以至于许多中国人都想学习；三是他能够运用四书五经来宣讲天主教的教义；四是他的自然科学知识让中国人佩服。

1601年，利玛窦进入北京。他在京城内广泛结交士大夫，一方面继续传播西方科学知识，另一方面也常与宾客谈论天主、灵魂、天堂、地狱等问题，努力在士人阶层中传教。到1605年，北京已有200人信奉天主教，其中包括徐光启等数名公卿大臣。

除徐光启外，李之藻是利玛窦在京交往的另一位重要朝臣。李之藻从利玛窦那里学会了制作各种日晷、星盘，于1607年写成《浑盖通宪图说》一书，介绍欧洲天文学知识。他还与利玛窦合作编译了《同文算指》、《圜容较义》两部重要的数学著作。为了加入天主教，李之藻甚至突破了中国长久以来的一夫多妻制度，与自己的妾室解除了关系。

doctrine. Fourth, the Chinese admired his knowledge in the natural sciences.

Other than Xu Guangqi, Li Zhizao was another important court official that Matteo Ricci had befriended. From Matteo Ricci, Li Zhizao learnt to make all sorts of sundials, astrolabes, and in 1607, wrote a book that introduced Western astronomy. He also collaborated on a couple of important mathematical works with Matteo Ricci. In order to become a Catholic, Li Zhizao broke a long-time tradition of polygamy in China, marrying only one wife.

Through interacting with these friends and with their cooperation, Matteo Ricci was able to introduce to the Chinese people, many Western scientific techniques and knowledge. At the request of Matteo Ricci, the Jesuits sent a large volume of European books to China, injecting into the Chinese society with an atmosphere of Western science and learning. Today, many of these books are still kept in the National Library in Beijing.

Concurrently, Matteo Ricci believed that he should introduce the finest of China's cultural world to Europe, in order for the West to learn more about this mystical country. He felt that the distillate of China's cultural works was concentrated in the "Four Books and Five Classics of Confucianism." (The Four Books refer to *The Analects of Confucius*, *Mencius*, the *Great Learning*, and the

穿儒服的传教士

通过与这些朋友的交往与合作，利玛窦向中国人介绍了很多西方的科学技术知识。应利玛窦的要求，罗马耶稣会还寄来了大量的欧洲书籍，将西方科学的新风气带到中国。直到今天，我们还能在中国国家图书馆里看到一些当时寄来的欧洲书籍。

与此同时，利玛窦觉得，应该把古老中国的文化精髓介绍给欧洲，让西方世界更加了解这个神奇的国

上海光启公园里的徐光启与利玛窦雕像。
Statues of Xu Guangqi and Matteo Ricci in Shanghai Guangqi Park.

Missionary in Confucian Garb

2007年，徐光启后裔和利玛窦后裔相聚中国上海，再续他们的先辈在400多年前结下的美好友谊。
In 2007, descendants of Xu Guangqi and Matteo Ricci gathered in Shanghai, China, establishing a beautiful friendship forged by their ancestors 400 years ago.

Doctrine of the Mean. The Five Classics of Confucianism include the *Book of Songs*, the *Book of History*, the *Classics of Rites*, the *Book of Changes*, and the *Spring and Autumn Annals*.) Hence, he planned to translate all these classics into Western languages, but owing to physical limitation, he only managed to translate the "Four Books" into Latin. In his later years, he wrote a memoir about his 30 years in China as a Jesuit missionary. Along with the Chinese classics that he had translated, they enabled the West to have a better understanding of China's ancient cultures, and opened a window into the sights and sounds of 16th and 17th century China.

度。他认为,中国文化最集中的体现莫过于四书五经(四书指《论语》、《孟子》、《大学》、《中庸》,五经指《诗经》、《尚书》、《礼记》、《周易》、《春秋》,均为儒家经典书籍)。因此,利玛窦计划把四书五经都翻译成西方语言。由于精力所限,最后他只将四书翻译成了拉丁文。

晚年,利玛窦总结自己在中国近30年的传教经历,写成回忆录。他翻译的中国经典和他的回忆录,让西方更深入地了解了古老的中国文化,以及16世纪末17世纪初的中国风貌。

VI

Burial in Beijing

In 1610, the overworked Matteo Ricci finally fell seriously ill. He seemed to have a premonition that of his own death, and had completed his memoir a few months earlier. He had also arranged all his important documents neatly and appointed Nicholas Longobardi as his successor.

On 11 May 1610, Matteo Ricci, a great man sent by the Jesuits from a land faraway, passed away peacefully in Beijing.

Ever since he stepped foot on China in 1582, Matteo Ricci had never left the country. When he first arrived in China, Catholicism was unheard of in China. By the time he died, the Catholic mission had made significant achievements and was a far cry from what it used to be like 28 years ago. With the hard work and dedication of Matteo Ricci and other Jesuit priests, many churches were built across China, attracted over 2,500 followers, among which were imperial court officials, well-known scholars,

6

赐葬北京，永留中华

1610年，殚精竭虑的利玛窦终于一病不起。他似乎对自己即将魂归天国早有预感。几个月前，他就尽力把回忆录写完了，还把重要的文件都整理好，指定龙华民（Nicholas Longobardi）担任耶稣会中国传教团的下一任接班人，同时对今后的传教工作留下了指示。

1610年5月11日，这位为天主教远来中国奉献了一生的伟大人物，安然地走向了生命的尽头。

自从1582年踏上中国的土地后，利玛窦就再也没有离开过。他刚到中国时，天主教在中国的传播可谓一片空白；他去世时，中国天主教事业已经是一片繁荣景象，与28年前相比有着天壤之别。在利玛窦和其他耶稣会士努力下，中国很多地方修建了天主堂，吸收了2500多名教友，其中不少是朝廷大臣、知名学

and even eunuchs. Yet, Matteo Ricci's contribution was not only confined to converting the Chinese to the Catholic faith, but also how the church had, through his determination and effort, taken root in China and prospered, occupying a distinguished place in society.

When he was alive, Matteo Ricci once hoped to build a cemetery for foreign missionaries, who had dedicated their lives to preach in China. Yet, this was an unthinkable idea in a time when foreigners were not even allowed to reside in Beijing. What was done, instead, was to send the bodies of the missionaries to Macau, and the mission would arrange for them to be buries in a public cemetery.

Matteo Ricci's colleagues kept his body in the church; they simply could not bear to dispatch his body back to Macau. At the same time, they wondered if the Chinese emperor would actually grant a special approval to allow a foreign missionary be buried in Beijing. Although the emperor had consented to Matteo Ricci a permanent resident status in Beijing, he had not specify that he could be buried here upon his death.

The funeral mass was attended by almost all the Catholics in Beijing. Among them was a famous scholar, who suggested that as long as the emperor decreed that Matteo Ricci could be bury in Beijing, he believed that it would be liken to legalizing Catholicism in China. As such the fate of Catholicism would not be determined by

穿儒服的传教士

栅栏墓地位于北京西城区阜成门外，1610年利玛窦去世后安葬于此地。后来它逐渐成为来华传教士及北京天主教徒的公共墓地。
The cemetery in which Matteo Ricci was buried in 1610. Located outside Fuchengmen in Xicheng District, Beijing. It later became a public cemetery of all foreign Christians Missionaries and Chinese Catholics who passed away in Beijing.

者，甚至连宫中的太监也不乏入教者。而利玛窦更重要的贡献，并不在于发展了更多的中国信徒，而是他凭借锲而不舍的努力，最终让天主教在北京、在中国扎下根来，并且开枝散叶，在明朝宫廷和整个社会都占据了一席之地。

生前利玛窦曾经希望能在北京郊区建立一处传教士墓地，安葬献身在中国大地的西方传教士。而在当时的环境下，外国人连住在北京都非常不容易，要想葬在北京，简直是天方夜谭。从前的做法是，外国传

the influence of an individual. If this really happened, it would be fulfilling Matteo Ricci's wish, and lay a smooth passage ahead for the Catholic mission in China. His idea was unanimously supported by all those who were present.

Being a highly regarded imperial official, Li Zhizao represented everyone and made a formal request to the emperor to bestow Matteo Ricci a plot of land in which he would be buried. His move was supported by many people, such as Xu Guangqi. Finally, Emperor Wanli made an exception and ordered for a plot of land in the countryside to be used for Matteo Ricci's burial.

With the emperor's blessing, the mission immediately proceeded to selecting a suitable location. Finally, the Jesuit priest spotted a suitable plot of land inside a monastery, located along Chegongzhuang in Beijing. The only monk who was residing was willing to let the missionaries have the land, as they had emperor's decree to back them. However, troubles soon arose once again.

The land, which the monastery was sitting on, actually belongs to a high-ranking eunuch, who was not friendly with foreigners. He refused to let go of the plot of land. The Jesuits was unaware of the details and proceeded to request the emperor to bestow them this particular piece of land, and was approved. Hence, with the royal decree in place, there was no chance to change the course of

教士去世后，将他们的遗体运到澳门，由教会负责安葬到集体公墓。

同事们将利玛窦的遗体停放在教堂。谁也不忍心违背他的遗愿，将他运回澳门。可是，中国皇帝会把墓葬的特权批给一位外国传教士吗？虽然皇帝允许利玛窦永远住在北京，却并没有说过他死后还能葬在这里。

丧礼弥撒开始了，几乎所有在北京的天主教徒都来了。他们当中一位有见识的名士提出，只要皇上能够下旨让利玛窦葬在北京，那么从此以后天主教在中国就能拥有合法的地位，而不再是由于传教士的个人影响而得到默许。这样的话，既能满足利玛窦的心愿，又能为中国的天主教事业赢得更好的形势。他的看法获得在场人们的一致赞同。

于是，身为朝廷重臣的李之藻代表大家向皇帝上疏，请求能在北京赐给利玛窦一块葬身之地。经过徐光启等人的共同努力，万历皇帝破例开恩，下令在郊区拨出一块土地用于安葬利玛窦。

有了皇帝的圣旨，教会立即去办理墓地的选址事宜。传教士们看中了北京城西的一所乡间寺院，寺

利玛窦墓园石坊门
The stone gate of Matteo Ricci's grave.

events.

With the assistance from the Ministry of Revenue that oversaw all property matters and the Board of Rites, the high-ranking eunuch eventually gave in.

A year later, after encountering so many obstacles, the first Catholic cemetery was established. The Jesuits built a chapel that was surrounded by an idyllic garden in an empty plot, and buried Matteo Ricci among cypress trees and bamboo bushes. Although he was a foreigner, his tomb took on the characteristics of the Chinese, and was elaborately decorated with a soaring dragon. The only difference was the crucifix that sat at the top of the

穿儒服的传教士

利玛窦墓墓碑,正面用中文和拉丁文刻着"耶稣会士利公之墓",反面记录了利玛窦生平。
Matteo Ricci's tombstone, on its front was the inscription in Chinese and Latin, "The Grave of Jesuit Priest Matteo Ricci," with a brief biography of Matteo Ricci at the back of it.

里只住着一名和尚。因为是皇帝御赐用作墓地,和尚愿意出让。可是,麻烦又出现了。

原来,这处寺院的产权属于宫中的一名大太监,而这个太监对外国人十分敌视,坚决不肯出让土地。传教士们由于不知详情,已经向皇帝请求下诏赐予这块地。如今圣旨已下,再想更改就不可能了。

通过主管土地的户部和负责管理外国人事务的礼部出面干预,大太监终于让步了。

几经波折,一年后,中国第一座天主教墓地终于落成。传教士们在原来的荒地上开辟了一个雅致的花园,花园的一端修建了一座六角形带拱顶的小教堂,

Missionary in Confucian Garb

gravestone, reminding people that the deceased was a devout Catholic. To show respect to the emperor and in memory of Matteo Ricci, many court officials attended the grand funeral ceremony.

This cemetery later became the burial ground of foreign missionaries in Beijing. Following Matteo Ricci, other Jesuit priests including Johann Adam Schall von Bell, Ferdinand Verbiest, and Giuseppe Castiglione were buried in this cemetery. The cemetery remains till today and is open to public.

金尼阁（1577—1629），法籍耶稣会士，明末两度来华，在华时间达12年。1615年，金尼阁在欧洲出版了他整理、翻译的《利玛窦中国札记》。

Nicolas Trigault (1577-1629), French Jesuit, who visited China twice during the late Ming Dynasty, and stayed in China for 12 years. In 1615, Nicolas Trigault published his translation of *The Journals of Matteo Ricci in China*.

In Matteo Ricci's memoir, he had recorded in detail, all that he had seen and heard in China as a Jesuit priest. He had fervently praised China's abundance in resources and prosperity, and had expressed a sincere love for the country. After his death, the Jesuit priest Nicolas Trigault translated Matteo Ricci's memoir into Italian, and entitled it *The Journals of Matteo*

又用四棵柏树和几丛青竹围出一片空间用作墓地。利玛窦的遗体入土为安。虽然他是外国传教士，但墓碑的外观还是入乡随俗，颇具中国特色，高大的汉白玉石碑上盘绕着飞腾的苍龙，只有碑额上镌刻着的十字架，提醒人们墓主人是位虔诚的天主教徒。出于对皇帝的恭敬和对利玛窦的追思，朝廷的文武百官都参加了隆重的葬礼。

这块墓地后来成为外国传教士在北京的集体墓地。继利玛窦之后，汤若望（Johann Adam Schall von Bell）、南怀仁（Ferdinand Verbiest）、郎世宁（Giuseppe Castiglione）等几十位来华传教士都葬在这里。今天，如果有人想凭吊利玛窦，还可以到位于北京车公庄二里沟的来华传教士墓地，去缅怀这位中西文化交流的伟大使者。

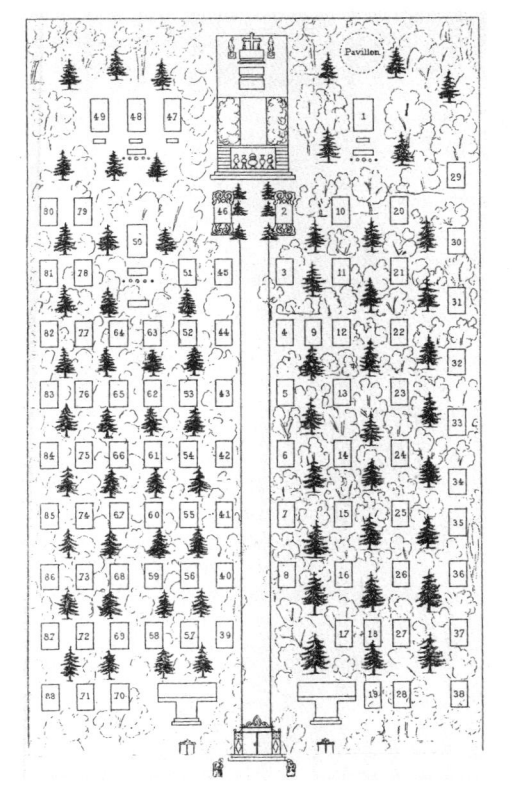

栅栏墓地示意图。这里先后埋葬了数百名西方传教士。
A diagram of the cemetery where a few hundreds Western missionaries were buried.

Missionary in Confucian Garb

Ricci in China. The book was hailed as a basic book for Westerners to find out more about China. Through the book, the life and times of Matteo Ricci in China as a Jesuit became known to many people in Europe.

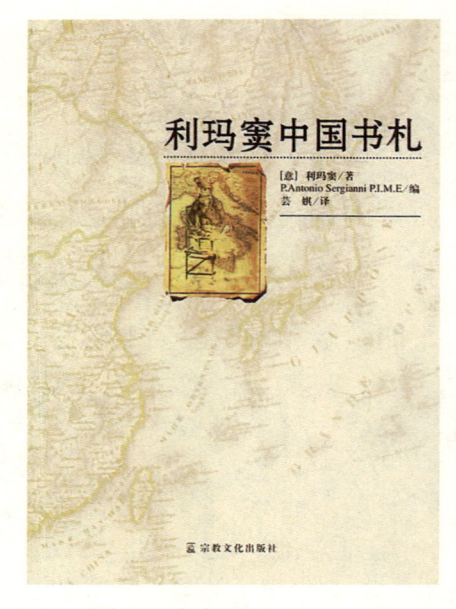

《利玛窦中国札记》中文译本
Chinese translation of *The Journals of Matteo Ricci in China*.

利玛窦在他的回忆录里，详细记录了他在中国的传教经历和所见所闻，极力称赞中国的富庶和繁荣，真诚地流露出对中国的深厚感情。在他故去后，耶稣会士金尼阁（Nicolas Trigault）将这部伟大的著作从拉丁文翻译成意大利文，题名为《利玛窦中国札记》，在欧洲出版。《利玛窦中国札记》被公推为西方人认识中国的基本著作。通过它，利玛窦的经历也为更多人知晓。如果想了解更多有关利玛窦的故事，你可以到这本他亲笔所写的书里去寻找答案。

VII

The Question of Rites

When Michele Ruggieri and Matteo Ricci first arrived in China, Catholicism in China was a blank slate, awaiting a long process of development. In 1584, there were only three Chinese Catholics in China. Until 1586, there were only.

As a heterogeneous religion that was entirely different from the traditions and culture of China, Catholicism had come a long way from Europe to change the mindsets of the Chinese and convert to Catholicism. However, for thousands of years, the Chinese had regarded Confucianism as a fundamental belief that is highly revered. It was a challenge for many conservative Chinese to consider changing this deeply entrenched belief. They were even worried that it would destabilize the root of the Chinese empire. Hence, when discussing his faith with the educated Chinese and scholars, there were constant oppositions toward Matteo Ricci as well. However, as he was protected by the emperor, and owing to the

7

身后困惑，礼仪之争

罗明坚、利玛窦刚来到中国时，天主教在中国还是一片有待开垦的处女地。1584年，信奉天主教的中国教徒仅3人，到1586年，中国教徒的人数也只有40人。

利玛窦进入北京后，由于皇帝给予他的特殊待遇，推进了天主教事业在中国各地的发展。1603年，中国天主教徒发展到500人。到利玛窦逝世的1610年，全国已有教徒2500余人。

作为一种与中国传统文化完全异质的西方宗教，天主教远涉重洋，到达几千年来一直将儒家学说作为正统思想的中国，并且想让中国人改变对儒学的尊崇，转而信仰天主教。对于当时中国的一些保守人士来说，这当然是一种挑战，他们甚至担心会因而动摇中华帝国的根本。因此，在利玛窦与中国开明士大夫和学者相谈甚欢的同时，反对利玛窦的声音也始终不

assistance provided by his friends in various places, these oppositions were simply heard but had not much effect on his work.

However, these oppositions took centre stage six years after Matteo Ricci died. The Catholic movement in China finally took a rough hit, which in history was known as "Nanjing Missionary Case." In 1616, The Minister of the Board of Rites in Nanjing, Shen Que, had on three separate occasions, presented his memorial to the emperor, denouncing the Catholics for encouraging the local people not to worship their ancestors. This was a major violation to the Confucian ethic of filial piety. However, all of Shen Que's protests were ignored by Emperor Wanli.

Undeterred, Shen Que sought help from an influential high-ranking official on the Board of Rites, Fang Congzhe, who advised him to arrest the foreign priests and imprison them, before seeking justice from the emperor. With the backing of Fang Congzhe, Shen Que wasted no time in putting the foreign priests behind bars. He surrounded the church in Nanjing, and arrested Alphonsus Vagnoni and Alvare de Semedo, along with over 30 followers. Then, an imperial decree ordered that all the foreign priests that were mentioned in Shen Que's memorial would be expelled to Macau. Hence, Alphonsus Vagnoni and Alvare de Semedo, along with Diego de Pantoja and Sabatino de Ursis, who were preaching in Beijing, were all

穿儒服的传教士

绝于耳。不过，由于皇帝对利玛窦的爱护，加之他遍布各地的有地位朋友的帮助，这些声音一直只是嗡嗡作响，没有形成气候。

利玛窦去世六年后，责难的声音占据了上风，天主教在中国的发展遇到了第一次较大的打击，史称"南京教案"。1616年，南京礼部侍郎沈榷先后三次向皇帝上疏，批评在华的外国传教士教导中国人不祭祀祖先，违背儒家学说中最根本的"孝"的大德。万历皇帝对沈榷的几次上奏都没有理会。

于是，沈榷找到一位有权势的同乡——礼部尚书兼东阁大学士方从哲，寻求他的帮助。方从哲给沈榷写信，建议先将这些在中国传教的外国人抓进监狱，

孟德高维诺（1247—1328），意大利方济各会传教士，1293年到达元大都（今北京），经元政府批准在大都宣教，奠定了天主教在中国传教事业的基础。

Giovannida Montecorvino (1247-1328), Italian Franciscan missionary, arrived in Yuan Dadu (now Beijing) in 1293, and was approved by the Yuan government to preach in the capital, laying the foundation of Catholic missionary work in China.

arrested and taken to Guangdong.

This case was no only restricted to the areas or Beijing and Nanjing, and many other places in China was affected by the outcome. The Jesuits in various parts of China began to handle matters tactfully, in order not to jeopardize the mission work that Matteo Ricci had put in place. However, compare to Nanjing and Beijing, the other areas did not take such a great hit.

During the case, Xu Guangqu, Yang Tingjun and Li Zhizao was among those who tirelessly went around helping the Jesuits, many of whom were hiding in Yang Tingjun's house. Xu Guangqi went on to writing the famous *Memorial on Distinguishing Learning*, which he presented to the emperor to defend the Jesuits and Catholicism.

In 1621, Shen Que was relinquished of his duty, and soon there was a revival of Catholicism in China. The Jesuits began preaching more openly, as churches that were once seized by the authority were returned to the Jesuits.

The conflict between the Catholicism and its opposition in China was soon resolved through the effort of the Jesuits, educated Chinese and the ordinary followers. However, the Catholic movement in China continued to be plagued by internal strife in Europe, and criticism from other denominations of the Catholic faith soon disrupted

再向皇帝请旨治罪。有朝中高官支持，沈㴶立即发兵包围南京的天主教堂，逮捕了在那里传教的耶稣会士王丰肃（Alphonsus Vagnoni）和曾德昭（Alvare de Semedo），还抓走了 30 多名教徒。后来，朝廷下旨，将沈㴶奏折上提到的传教士都驱逐到澳门。于是王丰肃、曾德昭，以及当时在北京的庞迪我、熊三拔（Sabatino de Ursis）等人都被押解到广东。

教案波及全国，各地的传教士大多谨慎应对，以保存利玛窦辛苦开创的传教事业。不过，被沈㴶直接告发的南京和北京教区还是受到了较大的打击。

教案期间，徐光启、杨廷筠和李之藻等人积极为天主教奔走。不少传教士都躲藏在杨廷筠家中，徐光启还写下著名的《辨学疏章》，上书皇帝，为在华传教士和天主教辩护。

1621 年沈㴶被撤职后，天主教又比较公开地恢复了在中国的传教活动，各地曾经被查封的教堂也先后由地方官员发还给传教士。

一场来自反天主教势力的攻击，通过来华传教士、爱教中国士大夫和中国普通教徒的共同努力，终于得到化解。然而，耶稣会士内部的争议、天主教其

the missionary work in China. Catholicism was finally banned for 100 years in China.

When Matteo Ricci first came to Asia, he was encouraged by his own vision of seeing thousands of people converting to Catholicism in a single day. He yearned to see that day come true. However, over the decade that he was in Guangzhou, there was actually not much progress in the mission work. He did manage to have a better understanding of China through his interaction with different people in society. With his sensitive nature, he was able to perceive Chinese culture with a serious attitude, and improved on his methods of preaching, and pondered ways to bridge the difference between Western and Chinese civilization. It was such thoughts that enabled him to befriend many high-level Chinese intellectuals, and began his mission work amongst them. His ability to win the hearts of the emperor, scholars, officials, and the eunuchs had also enhanced the popularity of the Catholic faith, along with his very own reputation.

Living amidst a culturally rich atmosphere and a systematic society, Matteo Ricci realized that his primary task in his mission work in China, was not to convert the masses and baptize them. Instead, his role was to establish a credible role for Catholicism in the lives of the Chinese people. Failing to achieve this would most probably have

17世纪西方绘画作品,描绘了最早进入东方的耶稣会士沙勿略(1506—1552)在传教过程中遭遇的艰辛和苦难。
A 17th-century Western painting that depicts the difficulties and sufferings faced by the Jesuit Francois Xavier (1506-1552), who came first to the East to conduct missionary work.

他修会对耶稣会在中国传教方针的责难、各修会间的利益争夺,却最终中断了利玛窦和他的伙伴们孜孜以求的"中华归主"事业,使中国的天主教传播进入了"百年禁教"的冰河期。

利玛窦初到亚洲时,也曾被一日归化成百上千人的梦想鼓舞,期盼自己能早日置身于这种景象之中。

the Jesuits cast out of China by government officials that were against their faith.

Because of such consideration, Matteo Ricci assimilated himself thoroughly into the Chinese society, adopting all things that were Chinese in his daily lives, actions, and speech. He not only put on the outfit of a Confucius scholar, but he also went further to keep a long thick beard, and hired servants. And when he went about, he would ride on a sedan chair, as walking was considered of low social status. All this was done in accordance to what the Chinese considered status in their society. He also found that many Chinese intellectuals were not concerned about their spirituality, and thus showed them scientific gadgets to make them interested in discussing about science, and relating scientific achievements to Catholicism, thereby slowly introducing them to the religion.

Matteo Ricci had employed an adaptation approach in his mission work in China. What it meant was to assimilate into the mainstream of Chinese society which centered on Confucianism, and slowly integrate and inculcate Catholicism among the Chinese people. As a predecessor of this approach, he was aware that Confucianism was a basic ideology among the intellectual people and scholars. In order to succeed in inculcating Catholicism in China's society, it must blend in well with

1552年，第一个进入中国的耶稣会士沙勿略在孤独中病逝于广东上川岛。
In 1552, Francois Xavier, the first Jesuit who came to preach in China, died in solitude on Shangchuan Island in Guangdong.

然而在广东的十几年里，传教事业并没有多大进展。在与中国社会各阶层广泛接触的过程中，利玛窦对中国有了进一步的认识。凭借一种逐渐增强的敏感性，他日益严肃地对待中国文化，重新思考传教的方式，以及怎样顺应与西方文明不同的中华文明。正是这些思索，使他后来能结识那么多的中国高层知识分子，潜心在学者群中开展缓慢、耐心的工作，在皇帝、士

Missionary in Confucian Garb

Confucianism. Hence, he dedicated effort in studying all the Chinese classics and Confucian concepts of righteousness and morals, so as to make use of them to explain the Catholic doctrine. As such, many of his published works were regarded as Confucian texts, which conformed to the taste of the Chinese scholars, making them more acceptable.

中国籍耶稣会士游文辉绘《利玛窦像》。这幅画像由金尼阁带回罗马，至今保存于罗马耶稣会总部。
Chinese Jesuit You Wenhui's painting of Matteo Ricci's portrait. After Nicolas Trigault took it back to Rome, it was kept in the Jesuit headquarters in Rome.

In handling the Chinese intellectuals, Matteo Ricci had adopted the same attitude. Regarded as the three pillars of China's Catholicism, Xu Guangqi, Li Zhizao, and Yang Tingjun were converted to Catholicism upon carefully studying its doctrine, and they concluded that it was not in conflict with Confucianism. For instance, Xu Guangqi still retained much of his Confucian lifestyle. All these scholars believed that Catholicism could be regarded as a supplement to Confucianism. Contrary to what the opposition believed in, Catholicism was not in conflict

大夫和宦官之间游刃有余，从而使耶稣会在中国的传教事业逐渐发展壮大。

在中国文化氛围和制度环境中待得越久，利玛窦越发清楚地认识到：自己的首要任务不是去大量感化教徒，给他们施洗，而是使天主教在中国人的生活中赢得一个能够被接受的位置。如果不能实现这一点，教会始终会面临被敌对的官员驱逐出中国的危险。

所以，利玛窦在衣食住行、言谈举止等各个方面全面"中国化"，让自己像有地位的中国人那样生活。他不仅穿儒士的丝质长袍，还模仿儒士蓄起长须、雇佣仆人。由于中国的上流阶层认为徒步出行是没有身份的人的作为，后来利玛窦出门也坐轿子。当利玛窦发现中国的文人儒士一般都很少关心宗教的灵魂层面时，他便向有影响的人物展示和赠送西方科技物品，试图加强与他们的联络，利用西方科学把他们吸引到天主教上来。

利玛窦的传教路线被称为"适应路线"，也称"合儒路线"。"合儒"就是亲近中国文化的主流，采取一种合而不同、求同存异的方式传播西方宗教。利玛窦是"合儒路线"的先行者。他意识到，儒学是

Missionary in Confucian Garb

to Confucianism, and was worth assimilating it into the mainstream.

In fact, for 28 years in China, making friends, adopting Confucianism and introducing his friends to science were all part of his tactics to preach Catholicism, which was his primary objective. But as he got closer to the state of affairs in the country, and employed a slow and steady approach in preaching, many people in Europe felt he had forgotten his main objective in spreading Christianity.

17世纪初福建泉州出土的天主教石刻，反映了当时天主教在中国的发展。
An early 17th-century Catholic stone carving unearthed in Quanzhou, Fujian Province, reflecting the development of Catholic missionary in China at that time.

Shortly after Matteo Ricci died, his successor Nicholas Longobardi, who had always felt that Matteo Ricci's approach in spreading the gospel was too conservative, initiated a more aggressive approach to speed up the mission work in China. He submitted his ideas to the Chairman of the Jesuits. Initially, the discussion was only an internal issue within the Jesuits themselves. However, Catholic factions that

中国士大夫安身立命之本，要想使天主教在中国扎根，一定要让天主教教义和儒学融合在一起。因此他致力于对中国文化的研究，熟读四书五经，并用儒家的仁、义等概念来解释天主教伦理。他写出来的著作因而被人们认为是儒书，投合中国士人的欣赏口味，使他们愿意去阅读、去接纳。

在对待中国知识分子时，他采取的也是同样的态度。被称为中国天主教"三大柱石"的徐光启、李之藻、杨廷筠，他们之所以信奉天主教，是因为他们认为天主教和孔孟儒学互相并不矛盾冲突。以徐光启为例，虽然他加入了天主教，但他身上同时也保留着儒家文化的深厚熏染。在他看来，天主教的作用在于可以"补儒易佛"。李之藻、杨廷筠也有类似的言论，认为天主教教义是符合儒家学说宗旨的，并非异端邪说。

其实利玛窦一生在华28年，介绍科学、交友合儒都只是手段而已，他的根本目的当然还是要传播天主教。不过，他努力去贴近中国的国情，做法比较稳健，以至于被有些人误认为他已经忘却了传教的根本。

利玛窦去世后不久，他的继任龙华民认为利玛窦

were displeased by the success of the Jesuits in China, and the special treatments they received from the Pope, began to formally criticize the Jesuits, targeting especially Matteo Ricci's adaptation approach.

Matteo Ricci had greatly admired the highly advanced Chinese civilization. He had made this clear in his memoir. In his mission work in China, he had tried his best to respect China's traditions and culture, as well as their customs and lifestyle. However, his approach was controversial to the Catholic Church and caused endless debates. For instance, Jesus was originally naked when he was crucified, but the Chinese felt that it was inappropriate to bare one's body in public, and to be barefooted was to be an outcast in society. To the Chinese, it was disrespectful to leave someone that was highly revered to go without clothes or shoes. Hence, when the Chinese artists painted the Passion of Christ, they would add shoes to Him and his disciples. The Franciscan priest Antonio de Santa Maria Caballero felt that such paintings were blasphemous, and they should not be tolerated. He then proceeded to send his protests to Europe, accusing that the Jesuits had employed inappropriate means in carrying out their missionary work. The Jesuits retaliated by send their priests to Europe to defend themselves. All these conflict accumulated to what was known as the "Question of Rites."

的传教方式过于保守,主张采取更多激进措施,加快在中国传教的步伐。他把这些意见上报给耶稣会总会长。本来,讨论只局限在耶稣会内部。可欧洲的一些古老修会,如方济各会、多明我会,对于耶稣会这样的新兴修会在中国的成功一直不满,而教皇又规定耶稣会享有在中国传教的特权。借着耶稣会内部意见分化的机会,这些修会将他们对利玛窦"适应路线"的抨击上报给教廷。

对于高度发达的中华文明,利玛窦始终非常景仰,并在他的著作中明确表明了这种态度。在中国传教的过程中,他会尽量去契合中国的文化传统和中国人的风俗习惯。可他的做法在教会内部引起了很大争议。比如,耶稣被钉在十字架上是裸体的,没有穿衣服,还赤着脚,而中国人认为,不穿衣服有伤风化,不穿鞋子的人没有身份地位,如果自己要去敬仰的人既不穿衣服也不穿鞋子,未免太悲惨太不雅观了。所以中国人在画耶稣受难像等宗教画时,就会给耶稣和其他赤脚的使徒画上鞋子。方济各会士利安当(Antonio de Santa Maria Caballero)看到这样的画像时,便觉得这是对基督的亵渎,不能容忍,并把严

耶稣会士利玛窦和汤若望,他们正展开一幅中国地图。他们的上方,是两位耶稣会的创始人。
Jesuits Matteo Ricci and Adam Schall von Bell, who were composing a map of China. At the top were two founders of the Jesuits.

The center of this controversy on divine names and Chinese rites were focused on three aspects. First, the translation of the name of Jesus Christ to the Chinese language; whether it should be translated phonetically, or follow the term "Shang Di," which Matteo Ricci used, and taken from the Chinese classic, the *Book of Song*.

厉的批评意见传回欧洲，指责耶稣会士在中国的传教方法非常不妥当。耶稣会中国使团又派人回去加以辩护，于是你争来，我辩去，就形成了"礼仪之争"。

"礼仪之争"的焦点主要集中在三方面：一是耶稣基督的名称在中文中究竟应该怎样翻译，是按照发音直译为"徒斯"，还是按照利玛窦的译法，用中国古籍中本来就有的"上帝"来表示？二是中国人对孔子的崇拜是不是偶像崇拜，儒家学说是不是宗教？三是中国人对祖先的祭奠，是只为表达对先人的追思，还是想寻求神灵庇佑的迷信活动？

在礼仪问题上，利玛窦原本也不同意中国天主教徒参加祭祖祀孔等活动。可后来他发现，中国人在祖宗牌位、孔子画像前行的叩头礼，和他们见到皇帝和父母等活着的人时使用的礼节是相同的。他领会到这些礼仪只是中国人的社会习俗，表示敬意的举动，并不是宗教仪式，所以开始允许中国教徒祭祖祭孔。而这恰恰成为后来其他修会指责他的重要理由。

"礼仪之争"中，很多在中国传教的耶稣会士被派回罗马教廷为自己的修会辩护。他们返回欧洲后，一方面著书立说介绍中国文化，一方面广交社会

On the question of rites, Matteo Ricci was originally against the idea of the Chinese Catholics taking part in ancestor worships and rituals. However, as he got to know about the customs and rituals of the Chinese, he found that bowing to the ancestral tablet and a portrait of Confucius was the same as their daily practice of bowing to the emperor and their parents. He understood then that such rites were all part of social customs that denoted respect, which had no religious connotations. So, he allowed the Chinese Catholics to pay their respects to their ancestors and Confucius. Yet, all these facts were eventually used against him by the various Catholic denominations.

Owing to the question of rites, many Jesuits priests in China were dispatched to the Vatican to defend their order. These priests then remained in Europe, published books and introduced China to the Europeans. At the same time, they widened their social influence by mingling with people of high social status. Through these Jesuit priests, many important characters, such as Gottfriend Wilhelm von Leibniz and Baron de Montesquieu, began to take an interest in China and expressed their views about it. Such cultural exchanges soon enhanced the Europeans' understanding of China, and for a while, a "China Wave" swept across various parts of Europe, and the cultural divide between the East and West began to narrow.

穿儒服的传教士

耶稣会士利玛窦、汤若望和南怀仁。继利玛窦后，汤若望、南怀仁等一大批耶稣会士相继来到中国，进一步向中国介绍西方科学、文化、艺术，使西方文化第一次大规模传入中国；同时将中国文化介绍给欧洲，催生了欧洲18世纪的"中国热"。以耶稣会士为代表的入华传教士，成为中国和欧洲早期文化交流的重要中介和桥梁，在东西方文化交流史上留下了一份宝贵的遗产。
Jesuits Matteo Ricci, Adam Schall von Bell, and Ferdinand Verbiest. Following Matteo Ricci, Adam Schall von Bell, and Ferdinand Verbiest, etc., a large number of Jesuits arrived in China, and further introduced Western science, culture, and art to China, on a large-scale basis for the first time. At the same time, they introduced Chinese culture to Europe, and gave birth to the 18th - century "China Wave" in Europe. The Jesuit missionaries in China played and important role in facilitating cultural exchanges between China and Europe, and left behind a valuable legacy.

名流，与当时欧洲思想界许多重要人物如莱布尼茨（Gottfriend Wilhelm von Leibniz）、孟德斯鸠（Baron de Montesquieu）等都有过各种联系。这些文化交流活动大大加深了当时欧洲对中国的了解，在欧洲形成了一股"中国热"。地球的东西两端由此经历了一段初恋般美好的互相倾慕的时光。

罗马教廷几经政策变更，最终彻底否定了利玛窦的"适应政策"，禁止中国天主教徒祭孔祭祖。1720

After a series of policy changes in Rome, the Vatican completely rejected "Adaptation Policy," and prohibited the Chinese Catholics from worshipping their ancestors or Confucius. In 1720, Emperor Kangxi (reigned 1662–1722) of the Qing Dynasty (1616–1911) released an imperial decree, banning all foreign missionaries from preaching in China. Following the ban, all Catholic activities died down and soon halted, disconnecting China from the West altogether. Such an outcome of what Matteo Ricci had begun was not what he would want to see happening.

In 1775, the Pope dissolved the Jesuits. With that, the "Question of Rites" conflict that had sustained for over a hundred year came to a close. Within the one hundred years when Catholicism was banned in China, the Jesuits were almost completely forgotten in the country. All the rare items from the West went into oblivion. However, what remained were Western ideologies and scientific knowledge, which had left a significant impact on Chinese culture, and also a legacy of Matteo Ricci.

年，清朝（1616—1911）康熙皇帝（1662—1722在位）下令，禁止外国传教士在中国传教。禁令颁发之后，天主教在中国的活动被迫减少，逐渐停止了融入中国文化的步伐。中国接触西方世界的一座桥梁就此被截断，与世界联系的窗口又关上了一扇。1775年，教皇宣布解散耶稣会，持续100多年的"礼仪之争"拉下了帷幕。

相信这一切，是在中国苦心经营28年的利玛窦未曾预料到的，也是他绝对不愿意看到的。禁教的百年里，耶稣会在中国一度取得的辉煌成就几乎被人们遗忘，那些稀罕的洋玩意儿也早已湮没在历史的烟尘之中。不过，传教士们带来的西方思想观念、科学技术却或多或少地在中国文化中留下了印记。想到这一点，早已荣升天堂的利玛窦也应有所释怀、有所宽慰吧！

Matteo Ricci: A Model in fusing European and Chinese Civilizations

Matteo Ricci was one of the pioneers of the Catholic missionary movement in China, and was known as the "Father of the Catholicism in China." He was also the first Western scholar to study Chinese literature and classics, while actively spreading Western astronomy, mathematics, geography, and other scientific and technological knowledge to the Chinese people. The Chinese literati respectfully called him the "Western Confucian."

Pope John Paul II commented: "Father Matteo Ricci's biggest contribution was in area of cultural blending. He compiled an intensive set of Catholic theological terminology and rituals using the Chinese language so that the Chinese people could know about Jesus Christ, and gave birth to the Gospel and the Church in the Chinese culture... As Father Matteo Ricci was sincere in becoming a 'Chinese among the Chinese people', it made him a great scholar, and in the most profound cultural and spiritual sense, he was remarkable in integrating his roles as a priest and scholar, a Catholic and Eastern scientist, an Italian and a Chinese."

The famous German scholar Wolfgang Franke said that that Ricci was "the first ever outstanding cultural bridge between China and the West." Japanese scholars, and author of a Biography of Matteo, Philip Ping Chuan You said that Matteo Ricci was "the first person in the history of mankind to gather all the knowledge of the culture European Renaissance and the Chinese classics," and hailed him as the "first citizen of the world." The US Life magazine also listed him as one of the most influential character in the second millennium (1000–1999).

利玛窦：欧洲文明与中华文明融汇的典范

利玛窦是天主教在中国传播的开拓者之一，被誉为中国天主教之父。他也是第一位阅读中国文学并对中国典籍进行钻研的西方学者，同时还积极在中国传播西方天文、数学、地理等科学技术知识。当时的中国士大夫尊称他为"泰西儒士"。

教宗若望·保禄二世（Pope John Paul II）评价说，"利玛窦神父最大的贡献是在文化交融的领域上。他以中文精编了一套天主教神学和礼仪术语，使中国人得以认识耶稣基督，让福音喜讯与教会能在中国文化里降生……由于利玛窦神父如此道地的'做中国人中间的中国人'，使他成为大汉学家，这是以文化和精神上最深邃的意义来说的。因为他在自己身上，把司铎与学者，天主教徒与东方学家，意大利人和中国人的身份，令人惊叹地融合在一起。"

德国著名汉学家傅吾康（Wolfgang Franke）认为，利玛窦是"有史以来中国和西方之间最杰出的文化桥梁"。日本学者、《利玛窦传》作者平川佑弘称，利玛窦是"人类历史上第一位集欧洲文艺复兴时期的诸种学艺和中国四书五经等古典学问于一身的巨人"，并赞其为地球上出现的第一位"世界公民"。美国《生活》杂志亦将利玛窦评为公元第二千年内（1000—1999年）最有影响力的百名人物之一。